剑桥雅思

Cambridge IELTS In... Training Plan

风向标 Wind Vane

IELTS

剑桥雅思写作精练

◎杨 凡 编著

外语教学与研究出版社
FOREIGN LANGUAGE TEACHING AND RESEARCH PRESS
北京 BEIJING

图书在版编目(CIP)数据

剑桥雅思写作精练 / 杨凡编著 .— 北京：外语教学与研究出版社，2008.5
(剑桥雅思精练系列)
ISBN 978 - 7 - 5600 - 7519 - 8

Ⅰ. 剑… Ⅱ. 杨… Ⅲ. 英语—写作—高等教育—习题 Ⅳ. H315 - 44

中国版本图书馆 CIP 数据核字 (2008) 第 063662 号

出 版 人：于春迟
责任编辑：周春梅 韩晓岚
封面设计：刘 冬
版式设计：袁 璐 平 原
出版发行：外语教学与研究出版社
社　　址：北京市西三环北路 19 号 (100089)
网　　址：http://www.fltrp.com
印　　刷：北京京科印刷有限公司
开　　本：787×1092 1/16
印　　张：11.5
版　　次：2008 年 5 月第 1 版 2009 年 3 月第 2 次印刷
书　　号：ISBN 978 - 7 - 5600 - 7519 - 8
定　　价：24.90 元

* * *

物料号：175190001

前言

如何备考雅思写作呢？要谈这个问题，还要从考生在雅思写作中所欠缺的四个方面说起。考生在雅思写作中所欠缺的四个方面分别是审题、结构、思路和语言。这是雅思写作的四个评分标准，也是笔者提出的“四要素作文法”。

考生在审题方面常犯的错误是：没有抓住题目的讨论话题和提问方式的要点，造成跑题或遗漏了题目中的某些要求。考生在结构方面的问题是：自由式写法——想到哪儿，写到哪儿，条理性很差，结构混乱。考生在思路方面的问题是：无话可说，写不够字数；车轱辘话来回说；前言不搭后语，逻辑性差。考生在语言方面的问题是：词汇缺乏；语法错误较多；用词简单，句型单一，缺乏变化。在上述四个方面中，考生在思路和语言方面更为欠缺。

如何解决上述问题呢？要提高写作水平和写作成绩，掌握一定的写作理论和写作技巧固然重要，但更有效的办法是**仔细研读、背诵和模仿真题范文**。本书正是在这样的思想指导下编写而成的，包括一些写作理论和写作技巧的讲解，但占本书最大篇幅的是大量的真题范文，每篇范文都是 7－8 分的标准。对于重点范文，笔者进行了详细的分析说明，总结了范文中使用的高频词汇、高分词汇和高分句型。本书中的题目都是以前雅思写作考试的真题。在雅思考试中，题目是重复使用的，所以这些题目在大家实际参加考试时，都有可能遇到。背熟这些真题范文对雅思写作获得高分大有帮助。不过，每篇文章中所表达的观点都是笔者个人的意见，仅供考生参考。

在本书编写过程中，笔者参考了一些关于英文写作的书籍，在此对相关作者表示感谢。另外，在本书编写过程中，也得到了笔者的学生巩凌燕、宗丹、张薇、丁香、张倩、谢邦文和白鸥的帮助，在此向他们表示衷心的感谢。

祝广大考生雅思考试取得成功！

目录

第一章　雅思写作考试概述

一、雅思写作考试的重要性

对绝大多数考生来说，写作可能是雅思四门考试中最难的。但写作可以反应一个人的综合英语水平，它又是四门考试中最重要的，尤其是对准备出国留学的考生，因为决定是否录取你的人会特别关注写作成绩。比如，如果考生其他几门考得不太好，造成总分较低，不够学校的录取要求，但作文成绩却考了 7 分，那么，学校很可能会考虑录取该考生。相反，如果考生的平均分达到了要求，但作文分较低，如只有 5 分，学校很可能就不录取该考生。

二、雅思写作考试的要求

雅思写作考试部分要求写两篇文章，考试时间是 60 分钟。

普通类（General Training）写作的第一篇是要求写一封英文信，内容涉及咨询、抱怨、感谢、邀请、道歉、给出建议或提出申请等等，字数不少于 150 词。

普通类写作的第二篇要求写一篇议论文，内容往往涉及社会生活中的热门话题，字数不少于 250 词。

学术类（Academic）写作第一篇要求对图表进行描述、解释和说明，字数不少于 150 词。

学术类写作第二篇也要求写一篇议论文，字数不少于 250 词。

两篇文章的写作时间一共是 60 分钟，但具体的时间分配没有硬性要求。根据不同的字数要求、写作难度和占分比例，建议考生第一篇文章（信或图表作文）用时 20－25 分钟，第二篇文章（议论文）用时 35－40 分钟。考生在刚开始练习的时候，可以不受时间的限制；但要有意识地不断地提高速度，争取在考试前达到时间上的要求。

三、雅思写作考试的评分

雅思作文评分实行 9 分制，从 2007 年 1 月起，写作考试开始实行半分制，即考生的作文得分可以是 5.5 分、6.5 分等。两篇文章分别评分，互不影响。最后的得分是第一篇占 ⅓ 的比例，第二篇占 ⅔ 的比例。

每次考试，写作的平均分都不到 5 分，能取得 6 分及以上的成绩的考生不到 20%。这说明雅思写作考试还是有相当难度的。

四、其他要求

雅思考试要求用铅笔答题。大家在平常练习写作时，就应该使用铅笔，以便在考试时习惯用铅笔答题。

写作考试时，会发给考生一张试题纸和一张答题纸，考生注意要将作文写在答题纸上。考场上不提供草稿纸，而且考生也根本没有时间打草稿。

第二章　30 天备考雅思写作的建议

下面，以 30 天为例，给出如何使用本书准备雅思写作考试的建议。大家可以根据自己的备考时间作出调整。

时间	内容
Day 1	阅读第一章、第二章以及第三章中的“一、概述”。
Days 2 – 10	阅读第三章中的“二、辩论型题目写法一：五段论式写法”。
Day 2	仔细阅读并背诵 Topic 1 的范文。
Day 3	仔细阅读并背诵 Topic 2 的范文。
Day 4	仔细阅读并背诵 Topic 3 的范文。
Days 5 – 8	从 Topic 4 – Topic 24 中任意选择 4 篇文章，仔细阅读，背诵。
Days 9 – 10	从 Topic 4 – Topic 24 中任意选择 2 个话题，先自己用“五段论式写法”练习写作，然后与范文对照，最好能让身边的英语老师仔细修改一下。
Days 11 – 17	阅读第三章中的“三、辩论型题目写法二：对称式写法”。
Day 11	仔细阅读并背诵 Topic 25 的范文。
Day 12	仔细阅读并背诵 Topic 26 的范文。
Days 13 – 15	从 Topic 27 – Topic 39 中任意选择 3 篇文章，仔细阅读，背诵。
Days 16 – 17	从 Topic 27 – Topic 39 中任意选择 2 个话题，先自己用“对称式写法”练习写作，然后与范文对照，最好能让身边的英语老师仔细修改一下。
Days 18 – 22	阅读第三章中的“四、解释型题目的写法”。
Day 18	仔细阅读并背诵 Topic 40 的范文。

Days 19－20	从 Topic 41－Topic 48 中任意选择 2 篇文章，仔细阅读，背诵。
Days 21－22	从 Topic 41－Topic 48 中任意选择 2 个话题，先自己练习，然后与范文对照，最好能让身边的英语老师仔细修改一下。
Days 23－24	阅读第三章中的“五、混合型题目的写法”。
Day 25	阅读第三章中的“六、常用模板式句型”，从中选择各类句型共 20 句左右背诵。
Days 26－30	学术类考生阅读第四章。
Day 26	仔细阅读并背诵 Topic 1 和 Topic 2 的范文。
Day 27	仔细阅读并背诵 Topic 3 和 Topic 6 的范文。
Day 28	仔细阅读 Topic 10、Topic 11 和 Topic 12 的范文。
Days 29－30	从剩下的话题中任意选择 2 个话题，先自己练习，然后与范文对照，最好能让身边的英语老师仔细修改一下。
Days 26－30	普通类考生阅读第五章。
Day 26	仔细阅读并背诵 Topic 1 和 Topic 2 的范文。
Day 27	仔细阅读并背诵 Topic 4 和 Topic 5 的范文。
Day 28	仔细阅读 Topic 6 和 Topic 7 的范文。
Day 29	仔细阅读 Topic 8 和 Topic 9 的范文。
Day 30	就 Topic 3 练习相关写作，然后与范文对照，最好能让身边的英语老师仔细修改一下。

第三章　议论文写作

普通类和学术类的雅思写作考试的第二篇都是写一篇议论文，但每次这两类考试具体的作文题目却不同。学术类的议论文题目一般要难一些，但这两类考试的写作方法和评分标准都是一样的。

一、概述

（一）字数和时间要求

雅思议论文写作考试的字数要求在 250 词以上。字数不够会被扣分，所以建议考生一定要写 250 词以上。不管作文写得如何，首先要满足字数上的要求。但也要注意，一般不要超过 320 词。字数达到 250 词的要求之后，分数的高低就主要取决于作文的质量了，所以字数写得太多也没有必要，而且肯定会影响质量。

在考试中，考生没有必要一个一个地数字数。一般每行大约 10 个词，数一下行数就可以知道大概的字数了。实际上，评卷官也不会一个词挨着一个词地数，只是根据自己的感觉来估测大概的字数。

既然两篇文章的写作时间一共是 60 分钟，根据不同的字数要求、写作难度以及占分比例，建议考生议论文用时 35－40 分钟。

（二）命题内容

议论文的考试题目很多，但从内容上看，主要可分为如下 10 类：

1. 学生生活

(1) Nowadays it is difficult for university graduates to find a job. Analyse the individual and social reasons and offer some solutions.

(2) University graduates receive higher salaries than those who have a lower education. Therefore, some people say such students should pay all their tuition fees. To what extent do you agree or disagree?

(3) Some people think that examinations have some bad effects on both students and teachers. Some people say they do a good job in the evaluation of the students' performance. What is your opinion?

(4) In recent years, many young people decide to further their studies abroad. What are the benefits and drawbacks of studying abroad?

(5) Some people think that, in order to improve the quality of education, students should be encouraged to evaluate and criticise their teachers. Others feel that this will result in a loss of respect and discipline in the classroom. What do you think?

(6) When a student chooses the future career, what factors and whose opinions should he consider?

(7) Some people like different friends. Others like similar friends. Which kind of friend do you prefer? Explain why.

2. 家庭生活

(1) Should old people stay at home or be placed in nursing homes?

(2) Modern lifestyles mean that many parents have little time for their children. Many children do not get as much attention from their parents as children did in the past. To what extent do you agree or disagree?

(3) Nowadays, nurseries and kindergartens take care of children from an early age, so women can return to their work and children can get used to society early. Is this a good thing? What's your opinion?

(4) Corporal punishment has been practised in families for quite a long time. In recent years, people's attitudes towards this practice have undergone drastic changes. Nowadays many people strongly oppose it. Should corporal punishment be abolished?

(5) It is generally acknowledged that families are now not as close as they used to be. Give possible reasons and your recommendations.

3. 现代科技

(1) Some people hold that the development of modern science and technology leads to environmental pollution and energy shortage. What do you think?

(2) Computers do not help children to learn more effectively. On the contrary, their usage has a negative effect on both the physical and mental development of young people. To what extent do you agree or disagree?

(3) Nowadays the jet plane is considered to be one of the most important and influential inventions

in the world. To what extent do you agree or disagree with this opinion?

(4) What are the advantages and disadvantages of the Internet?

4. 媒体

(1) Some people hold that it is the television that alienates the relationship of family members. To what extent do you agree or disagree?

(2) Advertisements are getting their way into people's lives. Discuss the effects of advertisements on people. Should all ads be banned?

5. 动物

(1) Should experiments be conducted on animals for the benefit of human beings?

(2) Some people think that the amount of time and money spent on the protection of wild animals should be spent in improving the well-being of humans. To what extent do you agree or disagree?

6. 环境、资源和交通

(1) The only way to improve the safety on the roads is to give much stricter punishments for driving offences. To what extent do you agree or disagree?

(2) What are the causes of water shortages? Please also offer some solutions to deal with this problem.

(3) Moving large companies and factories with their employees to the countryside could solve traffic and housing problems in major cities. To what extent do you agree or disagree?

(4) Traffic jam is a problem in most cities all round the world at present. What causes the problem? Make some recommendations.

7. 传统与发展变化

(1) In some countries, the national traditional arts are facing extinction. Some people think that the government should support them. Do you agree or disagree? What should the government do?

(2) With the development of society, customs and habits have changed a lot. Is it a good or bad phenomenon? What's your opinion?

8. 政府

(1) Some people propose that smoking should be banned completely. What is your opinion?

(2) Some people say the government should not put money in the arts, such as music, opera and paintings, but instead, should spend more money on construction of infrastructure. Discuss.

9. 平等

(1) In some countries, sports and entertainment personalities earn higher salaries than other professionals like doctors, nurses and teachers. Why do you think this happens in some societies and do you consider it good or bad?

(2) Many females join the army in some countries. Some people think women should not be allowed to serve as soldiers. Do you agree or disagree?

10. 社会问题

(1) Should criminals be sent to prison or should they do something else as a punishment? Explain your opinion and give your reasons.

(2) Unlike other countries, the police in the UK do not carry guns. Some think this leaves citizens unprotected, while others consider it reduces the overall level of violence in society. Give reasons for both sides of this argument and state your own opinion.

(3) Differences between countries have become less evident. For example, nowadays the same films, fashions, brands and TV programmes are found worldwide. To what extent do you think the disadvantages of this outweigh its advantages?

(4) International tourism has become one of the biggest industries in the world. Some people think it unfortunately causes a lot of tension rather than understanding between peoples from different cultures. To what extent do you agree or disagree?

(三) 写作格式

雅思写作考试不要求写标题，所以在考试时，考生直接从正文的第一段开始写，不用写文章的标题，以免耽误时间。而且如果标题出现错误，反而弄巧成拙。

写作时，要注意分段，不要全文都写成一段。分段有两种格式：

1. 缩进式

这种格式，每段的第一行向右缩进去 4 到 8 个字母，段与段之间不加空行，与写中文文章类似。例如：

The problem of traffic jams in big cities is very common in developing countries and China is no exception. But as to how to solve this problem, people hold different opinions. Some suggest that, in China, we should give priority to the development of private cars, others argue that public transportation should be put in the first place. I am for the latter solution.

Firstly, a well-established public transportation system is far more efficient and economical than private cars. We all know that one car holds at most five people while one bus can hold at least 50, ten times as many as a car does. So to move the same amount of people we need ten times vehicles if we use private cars. The more vehicles on the roads, the more chances for traffic jams to happen.

Secondly, land is rare in cities and parking places for private cars occupy much more land than buses do. In order to provide enough parking for private cars, municipal governments have to cut the budget for roads. It is obvious that with less private cars we can certainly have more money and land to build longer and wider roads to reduce traffic jams.

Finally, many traffic jams are caused by traffic accidents. With more vehicles in big cities, the probability for accidents to happen is higher and hence more traffic jams. To develop public transportation in big cities means there will be less private cars and less vehicles. The result is clear: There will be less traffic accidents and less jams.

Based on the above discussion, my conclusion is: To solve the problem of traffic jams in big cities in China, the best way is to develop public transportation.

2. 齐头式

这种格式，每段的第一行不向右缩进，但段与段之间用一空行分开。例如：

In recent years, the Internet has been gaining its popularity at an amazing rate. It seems that anyone who knows little about the Internet is out-of-date and lags far behind the times. The Internet plays such an important role that it undeniably becomes one of the biggest concerns in the world.

Those who welcome the Internet hold that it brings us great convenience and efficiency. Firstly, we can send emails to our friends in other countries in a few minutes while sending a traditional letter takes us at least a week and costs much more. Secondly, we can make friends with people from all parts of the world. It overcomes the geographical barriers and makes the world smaller. Moreover, the Internet accelerates the flow of information and spreads education to all corners of the globe. We can have easy and quick access to the latest information worldwide.

While people speak highly of the Internet, its drawbacks shouldn't be neglected. For one thing, it leads to psychological problems. An Internet-addicted person tends to be isolated, self-centred and unsociable. For another, there is a sharp rise in the rate of cyber crime. More and more financial crimes are committed via the Internet. In addition, it also has negative impacts on young people because there are a lot of obscene and violent contents online.

In my opinion, the Internet has more disadvantages. It gives rise to people's mental problems. It results in various computer crimes. It is harmful to the growth of the youth. Something should be done as soon as possible to protect people from the negative effects of the Internet.

（四）写作命题形式

雅思写作考试从命题形式上看可分为三大类：

1. 辩论型题目（Argumentation）

题目给两件事或两个观点，或者是一件事或一个观点，供考生支持或反对。这类试题在考试中占 70% 左右。例如：

(1) University graduates receive higher salaries than those who have a lower education. Therefore, some people say such students should pay all their tuition fees. To what extent do you agree or disagree?

(2) Some people think that examinations have some bad effects on both students and teachers. Some people say they do a good job in the evaluation of students' performance. What is your opinion?

(3) In recent years, many young people decide to further their studies abroad. What are the benefits and drawbacks of studying abroad?

(4) Some people think that, in order to improve the quality of education, students should be encouraged to evaluate and criticise their teachers. Others feel that this will result in a loss of respect and discipline in the classroom. What do you think?

(5) Some people like different friends. Others like similar friends. Which kind of friend do you prefer? Explain why.

2. 解释型题目（Explanation）

给出一种现象，让考生说明原因或提供解决方法等。这类试题在考试中占 20%。例如：

(1) Nowadays it is difficult for university graduates to find a job. Analyse the individual and social reasons and offer some solutions.

(2) When a student chooses the future career, what factors and whose opinions should he consider?

(3) What are the causes of water shortage? Please also offer some solutions to deal with this problem.

(4) It is generally acknowledged that families are now not as close as they used to be. Give possible reasons and your recommendations.

3. 混合型题目（Mixed）

即题目中包含两个问题，一个是辩论型的问题，一个是解释型的问题。例如：

(1) In some countries, sports and entertainment personalities earn higher salaries than other professionals like doctors, nurses and teachers. Why do you think this happens in some societies and do you consider it good or bad?

(2) In some countries, the national traditional arts are facing extinction. Some people think that the government should support them. Do you agree or disagree? What should the government do?

下几节将分别介绍这三种题型的写法。

二、辩论型题目写法一：五段论式写法

对辩论型题目，本书介绍两种写法：五段论式写法和对称式写法。下面首先介绍五段论式写法。

（一）结构

五段论式写法的结构共分四段或五段，如下：

开头段
理由段1
理由段2
(理由段 3)
结尾段

如果只写两个理由段，就是四段；如果写三个理由段，就是五段，但统称五段论式写法。

（二）开头段

开头段一般写四句左右，大约写 50 词，它包括以下两方面的内容：

1. 引出题目，阐释题目；
2. 旗帜鲜明地说出自己的观点。

（三）理由段

在开头段之后，要写两个或三个理由段，来支持自己提出的观点。理由段是五段论式写法文章最主要的组成部分，是考生的写作重点。

每个理由段（argument paragraph）是由表达一个中心思想（controlling idea or central idea）的一组句子构成，包括一个主题句（topic sentence）和若干个支持句（supporting sentences）。

主题句（topic sentence）是表达理由段主题的句子，它用以概括段落大意（announce the main idea of the whole paragraph），要求全段其他文字都围绕它展开。

在主题句之后，要写若干支持句来支持主题句。

两个或三个理由段可以均衡分布，也可以有主有次。但要注意，每个理由段都要论述充分，不能相差太悬殊。

（四）结尾段

结尾段的通常写法：重申观点（+ 重申理由）（+ 提出建议或希望等）。

下面，看一些用五段论式写法写的雅思写作考试的范文。其中前几篇重点范文给出了分析说明。

Topic 1　彻底禁止吸烟

You should spend about 40 minutes on this task.

Write about the following topic:

Some people propose that smoking should be banned completely. What is your opinion?

Give reasons for your answer and include any relevant examples from your own knowledge or experience.

Write at least 250 words.

Sample Answer 1

Some people suggest that the government should ban smoking completely. Indeed, smoking is harmful to people's health and it violates the rights and freedom of non-smokers. However, in my opinion, smoking should not be totally banned for the following reasons.

Tobacco is a wonderful commodity to tax. It contributes much to the government's revenue. For example, the government of Britain collects enough from smokers to pay for its entire educational facilities. If smoking is banned, there will be a great loss to the government's income. In addition, more serious social problems will arise, such as unemployment, because tobacco industry employs a lot of workers.

Those who strongly approve of the ban lay too much emphasis on the rights of non-smokers. They ignore smokers' rights. Smoking is just a personal hobby and amusement. It is a kind of lifestyle. It is a stress reliever and can bring great pleasure to smokers. Furthermore, for smokers, nothing seems more difficult and painful than giving up the habit.

We must admit that smoking is detrimental to people's health. However, the harm that smoking brings to people's health is exaggerated. As long as we smoke in moderation, it will not do great harm to our health. In history, many famous people, such as Sir Winston Churchill, smoked and enjoyed a long life expectancy.

To sum up, I do not think that smoking should be completely banned. Tobacco industry makes much contribution to the national economy. Smoking brings many psychological benefits to smokers. Moreover, the complete ban of smoking will give rise to many social problems.

分析说明：

1. 结构

这是五段论式结构，一共写了五段。

第一段：先引出题目，最后一句话旗帜鲜明地说出自己的观点：不应该彻底禁止吸烟。

第二段：给出第一个理由，吸烟在经济上贡献税收，增加就业。

第三段：给出第二个理由，吸烟会给吸烟者带来一些心理上的好处。

第四段：给出第三个理由，反驳对方，指出吸烟对身体的危害被夸大了：只要适度，吸烟不会对身体造成很大伤害。

第五段：先重申观点，然后重申理由。

2. 高频词汇

suggest	/səˈdʒest/	*v.*	提议，建议
ban	/bæn/	*n.& v.*	禁令；禁止
completely	/kəmˈpliːtli/	*adv.*	完全地
indeed	/ɪnˈdiːd/	*adv.*	确实
violate	/ˈvaɪəleɪt/	*v.*	侵犯
right	/raɪt/	*n.*	权利
freedom	/ˈfriːdəm/	*n.*	自由
wonderful	/ˈwʌndəfəl/	*adj.*	极好的
commodity	/kəˈmɒdɪti/	*n.*	商品；用品
tax	/tæks/	*n.*	税
contribute to			为……作贡献
government	/ˈɡʌvəmənt/	*n.*	政府
revenue	/ˈrevɪnjuː/	*n.*	收入；税收
collect	/kəˈlekt/	*v.*	收款
entire	/ɪnˈtaɪə/	*adj.*	全部的
facility	/fəˈsɪlɪti/	*n.*	设施
loss	/lɒs/	*n.*	损失
income	/ˈɪŋkʌm/	*n.*	收入
serious	/ˈsɪəriəs/	*adj.*	严重的
arise	/əˈraɪz/	*v.*	出现
unemployment	/ˌʌnɪmˈplɔɪmənt/	*n.*	失业
employ	/ɪmˈplɔɪ/	*v.*	雇用
strongly	/ˈstrɒŋli/	*adv.*	强烈地
approve of			赞成
ignore	/ɪɡˈnɔː/	*v.*	忽视
amusement	/əˈmjuːzmənt/	*n.*	娱乐
lifestyle	/ˈlaɪfstaɪl/	*n.*	生活方式
stress	/stres/	*n.*	压力
pleasure	/ˈpleʒə/	*n.*	快乐
painful	/ˈpeɪnfəl/	*adj.*	痛苦的
give up			放弃
admit	/ədˈmɪt/	*v.*	承认

as long as			只要
cause	/ kɔːz /	*v.*	引起
make contribution to			为……作贡献
psychological	/ ˌsaɪkə'lɒdʒɪkəl /	*adj.*	心理的
benefit	/ 'benɪfɪt /	*n.*	益处
complete	/ kəm'pliːt /	*adj.*	完全的
give rise to			引起

3. 高分词汇

lay too much emphasis on...			太强调……
detrimental	/ ˌdetrɪ'mentl /	*adj.*	有害的
exaggerate	/ ɪg'zædʒəreɪt /	*v.*	夸张，夸大
in moderation			适度地，适量地
enjoy a long life expectancy			长寿

注意：高分文章（7分，8分和9分）并不要求每个词都是高分词汇。在高分文章中，出现五个左右的高分词汇就可以了。其他大量使用的还是高频词汇和普通词汇。

4. 关联词

写作时注意使用适当的关联词，使文章连贯。

（1）转折

- Indeed, smoking is harmful to people's health and it violates the rights and freedom of non-smokers. **However**, in my opinion, smoking should not be totally banned for the following reasons.
  确实，吸烟危害人们的健康，并且它侵犯了非吸烟者的权利和自由。**然而**，我认为，不应该完全禁止吸烟，原因如下。
- We must admit that smoking is detrimental to people's health. **However**, the harm that smoking brings to people's health is exaggerated.
  我们必须承认吸烟对人们的健康是有害的。**然而**，吸烟给人们健康带来的伤害被夸大了。

（2）举例

- Tobacco is a wonderful commodity to tax. It contributes much to the government's revenue. **For example**, the government of Britain collects enough from smokers to pay for its entire educational facilities.
  烟草是极好的纳税商品，它对政府的税收贡献很大。**例如**，英国政府从吸烟者身上征收到足够的钱用于支付全部的教育设施。

（3）并列/递进

- If smoking is banned, there will be a great loss to the government's income. **In addition**, more serious social problems will arise, such as unemployment, because tobacco industry employs a lot of workers.
  如果禁止吸烟，政府将会损失一大笔收入。**另外**，还将会出现更严重的社会问题，如失业，因为烟草行业雇用了大量的工人。
- Smoking brings many psychological benefits to smokers. **Moreover**, the complete ban of smoking will give rise to many social problems.
  吸烟带给吸烟者很多心理上的益处。**而且**，完全禁烟可能会引起很多的社会问题。

（4）总结

- **To sum up**, I do not think that smoking should be completely banned.
  总而言之，我不认为应该完全禁止吸烟。

5. 高分句型

文章中高分句型很多，限于篇幅，只选择其中几句为大家分析一下。

（1）Indeed, smoking is harmful to people's health and it violates the rights and freedom of non-smokers.
确实，吸烟危害人们的健康，并且它侵犯了非吸烟者的权利和自由。

句型分析：
这是一个并列句，陈述了对吸烟的一种观点，用词准确地道。

（2）Those who strongly approve of the ban lay too much emphasis on the rights of non-smokers.
强烈赞成这个禁令的人们过分强调非吸烟者的权利。

句型分析：
这是一个含有定语从句的复合句，those 是主语，who strongly approve of the ban 是主语的定语从句，谓语部分是lay too much emphasis on the rights of non-smokers。

(3) It is a stress reliever and can bring great pleasure to smokers.
它有助于缓解压力，而且可以给吸烟者带来极大的快乐。

句型分析：
这个句子包含并列谓语 is 和 can bring，内容充实，语言简练。

(4) Furthermore, for smokers, nothing seems more difficult and painful than giving up the habit.
而且，对吸烟者来说，戒掉这个习惯是最困难、最痛苦的事情。

句型分析：
这句话是用比较级的形式来表达最高级的意思。

Sample Answer 2

In recent years people's attitudes towards smoking have greatly changed. What was once seen as a sign of sophistication is now more likely to be regarded as a bad habit. Some people even suggest that the government should ban smoking in all public places. Personally, I would side with this opinion.

The first and most important reason is that smoking is detrimental to smokers' health. It is well known that there is a definite link between smoking and some serious diseases such as heart problems and lung cancer. According to a WHO survey, the life expectancy of smokers is 10 to 15 years shorter than that of non-smokers.

Smoking is a hazard to health which affects not only the smoker himself, but also all the people around him. It has been confirmed that even if we don't smoke, our health would be undermined just the same if we work or live in a surrounding where others smoke. In fact, the rate of passive smokers getting ill is higher than that of smokers. Therefore, to some extent, smoking violates non-smokers' rights and freedom.

Opponents of the ban claim that, as a wonderful commodity to tax, tobacco contributes much to the government's revenue. This may be partly true. However, it is the most short-sighted policy you could imagine. While money is collected in vast sums from tobacco industry, more money is spent on cancer research and on efforts to stop people suffering from the disease. In addition, smoking causes fire, which results in great loss of life and property.

In conclusion, I advocate the complete ban of smoking. If all smokers would break with the bad habit, our world will be much better.

分析说明：

1. 结构

这是五段论式结构，一共写了五段。

第一段：先引出题目，最后一句话旗帜鲜明地说出自己的观点：应该彻底禁止吸烟。

第二段：给出第一个理由，吸烟对吸烟者的健康有害。

第三段：给出第二个理由，吸烟对非吸烟者的健康也有害。

第四段：给出第三个理由，反驳对方，指出吸烟虽然能为税收作出很大的贡献，但政府要花更多的钱研究癌症和治疗癌症患者。而且，吸烟会引起火灾，这也会造成生命和财产的损失。

第五段：先重申观点，然后提出希望，但此段没有重申理由。

2. 高频词汇

attitude	/ 'ætɪtjuːd /	*n.*	态度
be regarded as			被当作是，被认为是
side with			同意，赞成
definite	/ 'defɪnɪt /	*adj.*	明确的
according to			根据
survey	/ 'sɜːveɪ /	*n.*	统计，调查
affect	/ ə'fekt /	*v.*	影响
confirm	/ kən'fɜːm /	*v.*	证实，确认
rate	/ reɪt /	*n.*	比率
passive smoker			被动吸烟者
to some extent			在某种程度上
claim	/ kleɪm /	*v.*	声称
short-sighted	/ ˌʃɔːt'saɪtɪd /	*adj.*	短视的

policy	/ ˈpɒlɪsi /	*n.*	政策
imagine	/ ɪˈmædʒɪn /	*v.*	想象
effort	/ ˈefət /	*n.*	努力
cure	/ kjʊə /	*v.*	治愈
suffer from			忍受，遭受
result in			导致

3. 高分词汇

sophistication	/ səˌfɪstɪˈkeɪʃən /	*n.*	成熟；老练
life expectancy			寿命
hazard	/ ˈhæzəd /	*n.*	危险
undermine	/ ˌʌndəˈmaɪn /	*v.*	逐渐损害（或削弱）
surrounding	/ səˈraʊndɪŋ /	*n.*	环境
opponent	/ əˈpəʊnənt /	*n.*	反对者
property	/ ˈprɒpəti /	*n.*	财产
advocate	/ ˈædvəkeɪt /	*v.*	赞成，拥护
break with			屏弃

4. 关联词

(1) 因果

- In fact, the rate of passive smokers getting ill is higher than that of smokers. **Therefore**, to some extent, smoking violates non-smokers' rights and freedom.
  实际上，被动吸烟者患病的几率要高于吸烟者的。**因此**，在某种程度上，吸烟侵犯了非吸烟者的权利和自由。

(2) 转折

- This may be partly true. **However**, it is the most short-sighted policy you could imagine.
  这或许有几分是正确的。**然而**，这是你所能想到的最目光短浅的政策。

(3) 并列/递进

- While money is collected in vast sums from tobacco industry, more money is spent on cancer research and on efforts to stop people suffering from the disease. **In addition**, smoking causes

fire, which results in great loss of life and property.
尽管从烟草行业征收到了大量的钱财，但是更多的钱被用于癌症的研究和癌症患者的治疗。**另外**，吸烟会引起火灾，导致巨大的生命和财产损失。

（4）总结

- **In conclusion**, I advocate the complete ban of smoking.
  总之，我提倡完全禁止吸烟。

5. 高分句型

文章中高分句型很多，限于篇幅，只选择其中几句为大家分析一下。

（1）What was once seen as a sign of sophistication is now more likely to be regarded as a bad habit.
曾经被视为成熟的标志，现在更有可能被视为一种坏习惯。

句型分析：
这是一个复合句，what was once seen as a sign of sophistication 是主语从句。整个句子用词非常准确，如 be seen as a sign of sophistication, be regarded as 等。

（2）It is well known that there is a definite link between smoking and some serious diseases such as heart problems and lung cancer.
众所周知，吸烟和某些严重的疾病之间有着一定的联系，如心脏病和肺癌。

句型分析：
这是一个复合句，it 是形式主语，that 引导的从句才是真正的主语。

（3）Smoking is a hazard to health which affects not only the smoker himself, but also all the people around him.
吸烟对于健康的危害不仅影响到吸烟者本人，而且还影响到他周围所有的人。

句型分析：
这是一个复合句，which 引导的从句是定语从句，修饰限定前面的 hazard。not only...but also... 连接定语从句中的两个并列宾语。

(4) It has been confirmed that even if we don't smoke, our health would be undermined just the same if we work or live in a surrounding where others smoke.

已经证实，即使我们不吸烟，但如果工作或生活在我们周围的人吸烟，我们的健康同样会受到损害。

句型分析：

这是一个复合句，it 是形式主语，that 引导的从句才是真正的主语。主语从句中还包含两个分别由 even if 和 if 引导的状语从句和一个由 where 引导的定语从句。整个句子结构比较复杂，但条理清楚，容易理解。

(5) Opponents of the ban claim that, as a wonderful commodity to tax, tobacco contributes much to the government's revenue.

反对该禁令的人声称，烟草是极好的纳税商品，对政府的税收有很大的贡献。

句型分析：

这是一个复合句，that 引导的从句是宾语从句。宾语从句中包含做状语的介词短语 as a wonderful commodity to tax。

Topic 2 电视疏远家庭成员间的关系

You should spend about 40 minutes on this task.

Write about the following topic:

Some people hold that it is the television that alienates the relationship of family members. To what extent do you agree or disagree?

Give reasons for your answer and include any relevant examples from your own knowledge or experience.

Write at least 250 words.

Sample Answer

As one of the most important inventions of the past century, TV is playing a more and more important role in modern life. However, some people are starting to worry about its side effects on families. I am convinced that the existence of TV has brought about alienation among family members.

First, watching TV occupies our time to communicate with our family members. TV provides a ready means of relaxation for people who spend their days doing routine and busy work. As soon as TV enters our home, most of our free time is controlled by it. What is more, the one-eyed monster requires absolute silence and attention. If any member dares to open his mouth, the others will order him to shut up immediately. Therefore, we communicate less with our family members.

Furthermore, families often quarrel over what programmes they should watch. Thanks to hardworking TV workers, we enjoy more TV channels and more colourful TV programmes. But a question has arisen: It is difficult for families to choose a channel that everyone enjoys because they have different interests. It is inevitable to give rise to quarrels among them.

In addition, some TV programmes can have negative effects on people's mood and behaviour. For instance, a person who watches too many idealised programmes may become unrealistic. Moreover, unhealthy programmes which contain obscene and violent contents may induce people's criminal acts.

In conclusion, I think that TV indeed has led to alienation among family members. We should be aware about the problem. Something should be done as soon as possible to protect the families from the negative influence of television. For example, we should reduce the time spent in front of the little screen and spend more time with our families together.

分析说明：

1. 结构

这是五段论式结构，一共写了五段。

第一段：先引出题目，最后一句话旗帜鲜明地提出自己的观点：电视疏远了家庭成员的关系。

第二段：给出第一个理由，看电视占用和家人交流的时间。

第三段：给出第二个理由，家庭成员争夺频道。

第四段：给出第三个理由，有些不良的电视节目影响家庭成员的行为。

第五段：先重申观点，然后提出建议和希望，但没有重申理由。

2. 高频词汇

invention	/ɪnˈvenʃən/	*n.*	发明
century	/ˈsentʃəri/	*n.*	世纪
play a role in			在……方面起作用
start	/stɑːt/	*v.*	开始
worry about			担心
side effect（常作side effects）			副作用，意外后果
convince	/kənˈvɪns/	*v.*	使确信
existence	/ɪgˈzɪstəns/	*n.*	存在
bring about			带来
alienation	/ˌeɪlɪəˈneɪʃən/	*n.*	疏远
occupy	/ˈɒkjʊpaɪ/	*v.*	占用
communicate	/kəˈmjuːnɪkeɪt/	*v.*	沟通，交流
provide...for...			为……提供……
as soon as			一……就……
enter	/ˈentə/	*v.*	进入
control	/kənˈtrəʊl/	*v.*	控制
require	/rɪˈkwaɪə/	*v.*	要求
absolute	/ˈæbsəluːt/	*adj.*	绝对的
silence	/ˈsaɪləns/	*n.*	安静
attention	/əˈtenʃən/	*n.*	关注
dare	/deə/	*v.*	胆敢
order	/ˈɔːdə/	*v.*	命令
shut up			闭嘴
immediately	/ɪˈmiːdiətli/	*adv.*	立即
quarrel	/ˈkwɒrəl/	*v.* & *n.*	争吵
thanks to			由于
channel	/ˈtʃænl/	*n.*	频道
colourful	/ˈkʌləfəl/	*adj.*	丰富多彩的
programme	/ˈprəʊgræm/	*n.*	节目
interest	/ˈɪntrɪst/	*n.*	兴趣
have negative effects on			对……有负面影响
mood	/muːd/	*n.*	心情

behaviour	/ bɪ'heɪvjə /	*n.*	行为
unhealthy	/ ʌn'helθi /	*adj.*	不健康的
contain	/ kən'teɪn /	*v.*	包含
violent	/ 'vaɪələnt /	*adj.*	暴力的
content	/ 'kɒntent /	*n.*	内容
lead to			导致
be aware about			意识到
as soon as possible			尽快
protect...from...			保护……不受……的（负面）影响
reduce	/ rɪ'djuːs /	*v.*	降低
in front of			在……前面

3. 高分词汇

routine	/ ruː'tiːn /	*adj.*	日常的
one-eyed monster			单眼怪兽（此处指电视）
inevitable	/ ɪn'evɪtəbl /	*adj.*	不可避免的
idealised	/ aɪ'dɪəlaɪzd /	*adj.*	理想化的
unrealistic	/ ˌʌnrɪə'lɪstɪk /	*adj.*	不现实的
obscene	/ əb'siːn /	*adj.*	淫秽的
the little screen			小小的屏幕（此处指电视）

4. 关联词

（1）转折

- As one of the most important inventions of the past century, TV is playing a more and more important role in modern life. **However**, some people are starting to worry about its side effects on families.
  作为上个世纪最重要的发明之一，电视在现代生活中扮演着越来越重要的角色。**然而**，有人开始担心它对家庭的负面影响。
- Thanks to hardworking TV workers, we enjoy more TV channels and more colourful TV programmes. **But** a question has arisen: It is difficult for families to choose a channel that everyone enjoys because they have different interests.
  由于电视工作者的辛勤劳动，我们喜爱的电视频道和有趣的电视节目越来越多。

但是，一个问题产生了：家人很难选择出他们都喜欢的频道，因为他们有着不同的兴趣。

（2）并列/递进

- As soon as TV enters our home, most of our free time is controlled by it. **What is more**, the one-eyed monster requires absolute silence and attention.
  电视一进入我们的家庭，就控制了我们大部分的空闲时间。**而且**，电视要求绝对的安静和专注。

（3）因果

- **Therefore**, we communicate less with our family members.
  因此，我们与家人的交流就减少了。

（4）总结

- **In conclusion**, I think that TV indeed has led to alienation among family members.
  总之，我认为，电视导致了家庭成员之间的疏远。

5. 高分句型

文章中高分句型很多，限于篇幅，只选择其中几句为大家分析一下。

（1）As one of the most important inventions of the past century, TV is playing a more and more important role in modern life.
作为上个世纪最重要的发明之一，电视在现代生活中扮演着越来越重要的角色。

句型分析：
这是一个稍微复杂的简单句，as one of the most important inventions of the past century 在这里是介词短语作状语，句子的重心在后面，全句的时态是现在进行时。

（2）If any member dares to open his mouth, the others will order him to shut up immediately.
如果哪一个家庭成员胆敢讲话，其他人会命令他马上住嘴。

句型分析：
这句话包含一个条件状语从句，open his mouth 和 order him to shut up immediately 写得都

很形象，用词准确地道。

(3) For instance, a person who watches too many idealised programmes may become unrealistic.
例如，一个人看了太多理想化的节目，可能会变得不切实际。

句型分析：

这是一个复合句，主语是 a person, who watches too many idealised programmes 是主语的定语从句，谓语部分是 may become unrealistic。

(4) Moreover, unhealthy programmes which contain obscene and violent contents may induce people's criminal acts.
另外，包含淫秽和暴力内容的、不健康的电视节目可能会导致人们的犯罪行为。

句型分析：

这是一个复合句，主语是 unhealthy programmes，which contain obscene and violent contents 是主语的定语从句，谓语部分是 may induce people's criminal acts。此句用词准确地道。

(5) For example, we should reduce the time spent in front of the little screen and spend more time with our families together.
例如，我们应该减少花在电视机前的时间，而花更多的时间与家人共处。

句型分析：

整个句子写得很好，有三个加分点。第一个是用 the little screen 来指代电视机，既用词多样化，同时也表达了贬义。第二个加分点是 spent in front of the little screen，是过去分词短语作后置定语。第三个加分点在于全句用了一个并列谓语结构，主语是 we，两个谓语部分分别是 reduce the time spent in front of the little screen 和 spend more time with our families together。

Topic 3 动物实验

You should spend about 40 minutes on this task.

Write about the following topic:

Should experiments be conducted on animals for the benefit of human beings?

Give reasons for your answer and include any relevant examples from your own knowledge or experience.

Write at least 250 words.

Sample Answer 1

Since human beings existed in the world, animals have always been accompanying us. They are of great help to humans in many aspects. For example, they help a lot in medical experiments. However, in recent years a growing number of people believe that animals should not be used for testing medical techniques and drugs. As far as I'm concerned, I would not go along with them.

Animal testing allows scientists to create and test new drugs. With the help of animal tests, we have found cures to many formerly fatal diseases. However, many new deadly illnesses appear every year and new treatments and drugs are needed to combat them. Many people argue that animal testing is cruel. In some cases, this is true. However, it would be much more cruel to let people die because there is not enough information about a disease.

Another reason why I advocate animal tests is that at present there are no other better methods to replace them. Moreover, not only would the costs of testing on humans be extremely high, but also it is brutal to test new drugs on children or adults. Therefore, animal tests are still regarded as the only reliable and feasible method.

Animals such as monkeys or rabbits which are used in experiments can be easily raised. In fact, they can be bred in laboratories artificially. In other words, there is a large supply of animals for medical research. Using animals in drug tests will not have negative effects on the balance of ecosystem. Furthermore, most countries set standards for animal treatment in tests, and laboratories have regulations to prevent cruelty.

Animal testing is needed in the world we live in. It is better that animals suffer than humans do.

分析说明：

1. 结构

这是五段论式结构，一共写了五段。

第一段：先引出题目，最后一句话旗帜鲜明地说出自己的观点：动物应该用于医学实验。

第二段：给出第一个理由，动物实验能够研究出药品和治疗方法。

第三段：给出第二个理由，目前没有别的办法来取代动物实验。

第四段：给出第三个理由，用于实验的动物易于喂养而且繁殖能力强，不会破坏生态平衡。

第五段：重申观点。

2. 高频词汇

accompany	/ əˈkʌmpəni /	*v.*	陪伴
in many aspects			在很多方面
a growing number of			越来越多的
go along with			同意
allow	/ əˈlaʊ /	*v.*	允许
with the help of			在……的帮助下
cure	/ kjʊə /	*n.*	治愈；疗法；治疗用剂
fatal	/ ˈfeɪtl /	*adj.*	致命的
deadly	/ ˈdedli /	*adj.*	致命的
illness	/ ˈɪlnɪs /	*n.*	疾病
appear	/ əˈpɪə /	*v.*	出现
treatment	/ ˈtriːtmənt /	*n.*	治疗；疗法
combat	/ ˈkɒmbæt /	*v.*	与……斗争；战斗
argue	/ ˈɑːgjuː /	*v.*	辩论，辩解
cruel	/ ˈkruːəl /	*adj.*	残忍的
at present			目前
method	/ ˈmeθəd /	*n.*	方法
replace	/ rɪˈpleɪs /	*v.*	替代，取代
similar	/ ˈsɪmɪlə /	*adj.*	相似的
reliable	/ rɪˈlaɪəbəl /	*adj.*	可靠的
feasible	/ ˈfiːzəbəl /	*adj.*	可行的

breed	/ briːd /	*v.*	繁殖
balance of ecosystem			生态平衡
set standards			设置标准
regulation	/ ˌregjʊˈleɪʃən /	*n.*	规定
prevent	/ prɪˈvent /	*v.*	避免
cruelty	/ ˈkruːəlti /	*n.*	残忍

3. 高分词汇

be of great help to			对……有很大的帮助
extremely	/ ɪksˈtriːmli /	*adv.*	极端地，非常地
brutal	/ ˈbruːtl /	*adj.*	残忍的
laboratory	/ ləˈbɒrətri /	*n.*	实验室
artificially	/ ˌɑːtɪˈfɪʃəli /	*adv.*	人工地

4. 关联词

（1）举例

- They are of great help to humans in many aspects. **For example**, they help a lot in medical experiments.
  它们在许多方面对人类都有很大的帮助。**例如**，它们在医学实验中帮助就很大。

（2）转折

- With the help of animal tests, we have found cures to many formerly fatal diseases. **However**, many new deadly illnesses appear every year and new treatments and drugs are needed to combat them.
  借助动物实验的帮助，我们已经发现了许多以前是致命的疾病的疗法。**然而**，每年有很多新的致命疾病出现，需要用新的疗法和药物来医治它们。
- Many people argue that animal testing is cruel. In some cases, this is true. **However**, it would be much more cruel to let people die because there is not enough information about a disease.
  很多人争论说动物实验是残忍的。在某些情况下这是事实。**但是**让人们死于某种不明的疾病则更加残忍。

（3）因果

- **Therefore**, animal tests are still regarded as the only reliable and feasible method.
  因此，动物实验仍被视为唯一可靠且可行的方法。

（4）解释

- In fact, they can be bred in laboratories artificially. **In other words**, there is a large supply of animals for medical research.
  事实上它们可以在实验室中进行人工繁殖。**换句话说**，有大量的动物可供医学研究。

（5）并列/递进

- Using animals in drug tests will not have negative effects on the balance of ecosystem. **Furthermore**, most countries set standards for animal treatment in tests, and laboratories have regulations to prevent cruelty.
  把动物用于药物实验将不会对生态系统的平衡产生负面影响。**此外**，大多数国家都对动物实验制定了标准，实验室也有相关规定来杜绝残忍的行为。

5. 高分句型

文章中高分句型很多，限于篇幅，只选择其中几句为大家分析一下。

（1）Since human beings existed in the world, animals have always been accompanying us.
从人类存在于这个世界上以来，动物就一直陪伴着我们。它们在许多方面对人类都有很大的帮助。

句型分析：

在此句中，since是连词，表示“自从”的意思，引导时间状语从句，主句使用的是现在完成进行时。层次清楚，意思明确。

（2）Another reason why I advocate animal tests is that at present there are no other better methods to replace them.
我支持动物实验的另一个原因是现在还没有更好的方法来替代它们。

句型分析：

主语是another reason，why I advocate animal tests是主语的定语从句，that at present there are no other better methods to replace them 是表语从句。

(3) Moreover, not only would the costs of testing on humans be extremely high, but also it is brutal to test new drugs on children or adults.
更甚的是，用人来进行实验不仅费用将极其昂贵，而且在儿童和成人身上测试新药也是极其残忍的。

句型分析：
not only...but also... 在这里连接两个并列句，当 not only 放在句首时，句子必须倒装，所以第一个句子用了倒装形式。

(4) Using animals in drug tests will not have negative effects on the balance of ecosystem.
把动物用于药物实验将不会对生态系统的平衡产生负面影响。

句型分析：
using animals in drug tests 是动名词短语作主语。

(5) Furthermore, most countries set standards for animal treatment in tests, and laboratories have regulations to prevent cruelty.
此外，大多数国家都对动物实验制定了标准，实验室也有相关规定来杜绝残忍的行为。

句型分析：
全句是并列句结构，set standards for 和 have regulations to 都用得非常好。

Sample Answer 2

Animals play an important role in the progress of our human beings. For example, such animals as monkeys or rabbits are used in medical research. Indeed, animal testing has dramatically improved the health of human beings human beings. Without animal testing, many patients would suffer from and even die of their diseases. However, despite these benefits, I believe that animals should not be used for testing medical techniques and drugs.

First, animal tests violate animals' rights. Although humans have been occupying the dominant position since they appeared on the earth, Darwin believed that human beings evolved from apes.

Therefore, man is also a member of animals. To some extent, man and animals are equal. Moreover, animals are of great help to humans in many aspects. Some kinds of animals have been used for transportation. Some others help the police solve cases. In modern times, some animals are raised as pets. However, in experiments, animals are usually killed or at least suffer from great pains. It is a kind of brutality and cruelty.

Second, not all experiments are necessary. Nowadays animals are used in too many experiments. Some diseases are not common ones and will not lead to people's death. Furthermore, with the fast development of science and technology, other alternatives have been found to replace animal testing. For example, computer simulation can achieve similar results.

And last, not all the experiments are reliable. Animals and humans are two quite different creatures. The treatments and drugs which are effective on animals are sometimes useless and can even have negative effects on humans. That is to say, information gathered from animals is not always useful to humans.

All in all, such kind of brutality should be halted. We should create a pain-free life for all animals.

分析说明：

1. 结构

这是五段论式结构，一共写了五段。

第一段：先引出题目，最后一句话旗帜鲜明地说出自己的观点：动物不应该用于医学实验。

第二段：给出第一个理由，这种做法侵犯了动物的权利。

第三段：给出第二个理由，并不是所有的动物实验都是必要的。

第四段：给出第三个理由，并不是所有的动物实验都是可靠的。

第五段：先重申观点，然后提出希望，没有重申理由。

2. 高频词汇

progress	/ 'prəʊgres /	*n.*	进步
medical research			医学研究
dramatically	/ drə'mætɪkəli /	*adv.*	极大地
improve	/ ɪm'pruːv /	*v.*	提高
human race			人类

patient	/ ˈpeɪʃənt /	*n.*	病人
despite	/ dɪˈspaɪt /	*prep.*	不管，尽管
appear	/ əˈpɪə /	*v.*	出现
at least			至少
common	/ ˈkɒmən /	*adj.*	常见的
achieve	/ əˈtʃiːv /	*v.*	获得
similar	/ ˈsɪmələ /	*adj.*	相似的
result	/ rɪˈzʌlt /	*n.*	结果
creature	/ ˈkriːtʃə /	*n.*	生物
effective	/ ɪˈfektɪv /	*adj.*	有效的

3. 高分词汇

dominant	/ ˈdɒmɪnənt /	*adj.*	统治的
transportation	/ ˌtrænspɔːˈteɪʃən /	*n.*	运输
brutality	/ bruːˈtælɪti /	*n.*	残忍
simulation	/ ˌsɪmjʊˈleɪʃən /	*n.*	模拟
halt	/ hɔːlt /	*v.*	中止

4. 关联词

（1）举例

- Animals play an important role in the progress of our human beings. **For example**, such animals as monkeys or rabbits are used in medical research.
  动物在人类的进步中扮演着重要的角色。**例如**，猴子、兔子等动物就常用于医学研究。

（2）转折

- **However**, despite these benefits, I believe that animals should not be used for testing medical techniques and drugs.
  然而，虽然有这些好处，我认为动物不应该用于测试医疗技术和药物。
- **However**, in experiments, animals are usually killed or at least suffer from great pains.
  但在实验中，动物却经常被杀死，至少也要忍受极大的痛苦。

（3）并列/递进

- **Moreover**, animals are of great help to humans in many aspects.

  此外，动物在很多方面对人类都有很大帮助。

（4）解释

- **That is to say**, information gathered from animals is not always useful to humans.

  这就是说，从动物身上得来的信息对人类来说并不总是有用的。

5. 高分句型

文章中高分句型很多，限于篇幅，只选择其中几句为大家分析一下。

（1）For example, such animals as monkeys or rabbits are used in medical research.

例如，猴子、兔子等动物就常用于医学研究。

句型分析：

such animals as monkeys or rabbits = animals such as monkeys or rabbits

（2）Although humans have been occupying the dominant position since they appeared on the earth, Darwin believed that human beings evolved from apes.

虽然人类自从出现在地球上起就占据了统治地位，但是达尔文相信人类是从猿进化而来。

句型分析：

这是包含让步状语从句的复合句，occupy the dominant position 用得比较好。

（3）Some diseases are not common ones and will not lead to people's death.

有些疾病并不常见，也不会导致人们的死亡。

句型分析：

全句是并列谓语结构。主语是 some diseases，两个谓语部分分别是 are not common ones 和 will not lead to people's death。

（4）Furthermore, with the fast development of science and technology, other alternatives have been found to replace animal testing.

另外，随着科学技术的发展，其他的替换方法已经找到，可用于取代动物试验。

句型分析：

介词短语 with the fast development of science and technology 作状语，全句使用的是被动语态的现在完成时态。

（5）The treatments and drugs which are effective on animals are sometimes useless and can even have negative effects on humans.

那些对动物有效的疗法和药物对人有时是没用的，甚至有副作用。

句型分析：

主语是 the treatments and drugs，which are effective on animals 是修饰限定主语的定语从句，主句中的两个谓语部分是 are sometimes useless 和 can even have negative effects on humans。

Topic 4 全民高等教育

You should spend about 40 minutes on this task.

Write about the following topic:

Some people believe that a college or university education should be available to all students. Others believe that higher education should be available only to good students. Which view do you agree with?

Give reasons for your answer and include any relevant examples from your own knowledge or experience.

Write at least 250 words.

Sample Answer

There is no denial that a college or university education is very beneficial. Those who receive higher education have more opportunities. They often hold better jobs, earn a higher income and enjoy a more comfortable and secure lifestyle. Unfortunately, places in colleges and universities are often limited and reserved for "good" students. It is my belief that this practice is not only detrimental to those students denied a college or university education, but to society as a whole. Therefore, higher education should be available to all students.

One reason that higher education should not be limited to "good" students is that not all secondary students study in equal circumstances. The facilities and teaching at some high schools are superior to those at others, and the students who study there enjoy a great advantage. In addition, a student's performance can be affected by his or her home environment or family financial pressure. It is often more difficult for a student from a disadvantaged environment or school to perform well. However, this does not mean that the student would not appreciate and benefit from higher education if given the opportunity.

Another reason for making higher education available to all is to encourage less capable students to improve. If students who lag behind in academic performance believe that they have no hope of entering a college or university, they may feel that there is no point in studying diligently. However, if they see a more direct link between their academic performance and their future opportunities, they will be more motivated. In this way, a poor student may turn out to be a good one.

Finally, a better educated population contributes to the growth and prosperity of a society as a whole. For this reason, it is advantageous to educate as many young people as possible. Furthermore, by denying higher education to students who do not gain good marks in their secondary education, the country may be ignoring a future Einstein. When every person in society is given the opportunity to tap his or her potential to the full, society will benefit.

For all of these reasons, I believe that higher education should be available to all students, not only to those with good academic performance in middle schools. Of course, it is desirable to encourage good performance of students. This can be done by offering financial support in the form of scholarships to those who work hard. In this way, we can ensure that students have the ability to take advantage of the opportunities available to them.

Topic 5 关注名人的意见

You should spend about 40 minutes on this task.

Write about the following topic:

When famous people such as actors, athletes and rock stars give their opinions, many people listen. Do you think we should pay attention to these opinions?

Give reasons for your answer and include any relevant examples from your own knowledge or experience.

Write at least 250 words.

Sample Answer

Famous people, such as athletes, actors, and other entertainers, are often interviewed by the media. They not only answer questions about their careers and personal lives, but also often give their opinions on issues of the day. The public tend to give more consideration to the views of the famous than to the opinions of more ordinary people. Should we give greater weight to their opinions? In my opinion, we should not, for the following reasons.

First, famous people are not necessarily well informed about the issues under discussion. While everyone has a right to express his opinion, a willingness to speak does not imply knowledge. Furthermore, a famous person may be an authority in his field, but that does not mean he is also an expert in other fields. For example, an actor who plays a doctor on TV is probably not a true authority on medical matters.

Second, a famous person may not be impartial. He may have financial or other motives for the opinions he espouses. This is particularly true when some type of product is involved. A good example of this would be an entertainer who advertises the goodness of a certain product while he has, in fact, never ever tried it.

Third, a reliance on the opinions of famous people may prevent us from thinking by ourselves. We should all develop the ability to evaluate facts and reach our own conclusions. Though there is no harm to listen to the opinions of others, we must realise that our situations are often very different. What may be true or beneficial for one person, may not be so for others. This is especially true in the case of famous people who, due to their wealth and fame, live in circumstances that are very different from those of ordinary people.

To sum up, it is better for us to learn to evaluate situations and reach our own conclusions than to rely on the opinions of others, no matter how well-known they are. Listening to the views of other people is a good way to gather information so as to make our own decisions. However, we should not accept the opinions of others blindly. Instead, we must consider their knowledge and motivation.

Topic 6 全球一体化

You should spend about 40 minutes on this task.

Write about the following topic:

Differences between countries have become less evident. For example, nowadays the same films, fashions, brands and TV programmes are found worldwide. To what extent do you think the disadvantages of this outweigh its advantages?

Give reasons for your answer and include any relevant examples from your own knowledge or experience.

Write at least 250 words.

Sample Answer

Globalisation creates conditions for widening international exchanges and strengthening mutual understanding between nations. It expands cultural, educational and scientific cooperation between countries. It encourages the process of modernisation and the enrichment of national culture. However, I believe the disadvantages of this outweigh its advantages.

Globalisation creates the possible danger of diminishing the national culture and exerts a negative impact on the preservation of national identity. Through globalisation and policy of reform and opening-up, different concepts, lowered ethical standards, individualistic lifestyles and harmful cultural products can easily be imported into one country. At present, modern information technology which is mainly controlled by US is hourly and intensively disseminating US ideology, way of life and culture across the world. Even US food is promoted so that some people consider globalisation as "global Americanisation".

During the process of economic globalisation, inequality between developed and developing countries has been increasing and the gap between the rich and the poor has become wider. Globalisation goes to assist developed countries. Globalisation does not pose equal interests and risks to all nations. With an overwhelming advantage compared with most of the developing countries in terms of finance and the level of science and technology, developed capitalist countries control the situation of economic globalisation.

For these reasons, globalisation is a fierce and complicated struggle in both cultural and ideological fields. As the proverb says, "Fire is a good servant, but a bad master." We have taken the initiative in global economic integration, but also have to take the initiative in fighting to prevent our distinct culture from crossbred phenomena.

Topic 7 国际旅游业促进相互了解

You should spend about 40 minutes on this task.

Write about the following topic:

International tourism has become one of the biggest industries in the world. Some people think it unfortunately causes a lot of tension rather than understanding between peoples from different cultures. To what extent do you agree or disagree?

Give reasons for your answer and include any relevant examples from your own knowledge or experience.

Write at least 250 words.

Sample Answer

International tourism has boomed to be one of the biggest industries in the world. What was once the "Grand Tour", only reserved for the rich, is now within most people's grasp. Some people think it would definitely improve the understanding of peoples from different cultures. However, I believe it causes a lot of tension instead.

The aim of most international tourists is for sightseeing. Their stay is generally too short for them to get more than a cursory glance. A strict schedule makes it impossible for the tourists to have a chance to communicate with local people. Even if they are lucky enough to be among the locals, language is always a barrier. Thus, any deep understanding about local cultures or communication with local residents is out of the question.

Tension arises frequently when international tourists are found to show disrespect for local customs due to their unawareness of local traditions or history. Last year, I, followed by a couple of friends, travelled to a small county located in Bolivia. Surprisingly we happened to see thousands of people singing and dancing on the street. Three guys dressed in local costume swayed badly towards us, bringing beer for us. Owing to our arrival in a totally new place, we declined to take any alcohol in case of being entrapped. Unexpectedly, quarrels occurred and one of them spat on us, whose behaviour turned our journey to be a trip of humiliation and resentment. As a matter of fact, the local residents were celebrating yearly Beer Festival. Our refusal was regarded as a bad manner to look down upon them.

Differences between people from different cultures have existed for a long time. Several international trips cannot solve the problem.

Topic 8 父母与老师

You should spend about 40 minutes on this task.

Write about the following topic:

Parents are the best teachers. Do you agree or disagree?

Give reasons for your answer and include any relevant examples from your own knowledge or experience.

Write at least 250 words.

Sample Answer 1

Obviously, the earliest teachers we have in our lives in most cases are our parents, and they are generally involved in the development and education of their children. Yet few of parents are good teachers in most cases, to say nothing of the best teachers.

First of all, as normal individuals, some parents more or less have bad habits. Even though parents almost instinctively devote themselves to cultivating their offsprings, the outcome might turn out to be disappointing, for many children tend to unconsciously or subconsciously imitate the example of their parents. Another deficiency of parents as teachers is the fact that most parents lack the common sense of education. All too often, we observe that some parents tend to pursue their own cherished but failed dreams by forcing their children to develop in a prearranged direction. Ironically, if their children do not follow the instructions, the children would be regarded as disobedient or rebellious. In fact, it is parents rather than their children that are virtually disobeying the common sense.

Moreover, even if some parents are qualified as good teachers, few of them are the best ones. When children are in the preliminary school, it is not surprising that parents are capable of teaching their children almost every subject even better than professional teachers in the school. But the situation will not last long. We live in a world where knowledge is accumulated by practice and at the same time becomes more and more specialised. Therefore, to be a professional in a certain field today takes a much longer time than ever before. No parent is able to be professional in all subjects, though they might be experts in one or more fields.

Parents may, nevertheless, help their children much more than some teachers do because some of children's education is virtually beyond teachers' reach. Psychological studies have shown us that parents' love sometimes has astonishingly magic power over their children. Albert Einstein's mother and Forest Gump's mother are both good examples. On the other hand, parents might also do their children more harm than bad teachers would. The natures of those children whose parents have divorced are often severely distorted. In a word, it is rather superficial to say that parents are the best teachers.

Sample Answer 2

Obviously, the first teachers we have in our lives in most cases are our parents. They teach us to walk, to speak, and to have good manners before we get into "the real world". Parents are generally more involved in the development and education of children than the professional teachers that we have in school.

Almost for sure our parents are the best teachers at the beginning of our lives, which actually corresponds to the parents' role in nature. Parents are undoubtedly devoted to their children; they are willing to sacrifice themselves for their children. They love us and have great patience while passing down their knowledge to us. They wish us success and thus will not teach us bad things. And of course, implicit learning occurs when children unconsciously imitate some of their parents' habits and styles of behaviour.

During the second stage of children's development—adolescence—parents can still be in the best position to offer advice, even though the children might not accept it. In this case, perhaps children's friends would be the best teachers. Adolescents are notoriously rebellious in many cultures and may automatically reject any advice from their parents. My first marriage, for instance, was solely a matter of doing the opposite when my parents tried to intrude by offering their advice. So to such matters, parents should be flexible, and try to be friends with their children. We can see that being the teacher of a growing child becomes more and more complicated as time passes, and many parents are simply not able to meet the increasing demands.

On the other hand, I would say that parents are not professional teachers and they tend to be biased in their love of their children. So wishing them good things and an easy life may prevent children from maturation. In addition, parents can only provide a limited number of world views to their children while education needs various world views from different perspectives to help children form their own views. Thus, when children go to school and have more than one teacher to learn from, they learn much more than their parents could probably give them. Furthermore, once our parents get older, they become more conservative and cannot always be objective with regard to modern trends and fashions. Thus we need to take their advice with caution during that period. However, I believe some kind of intuition is shared between relatives. And the great love which exists in families still makes our parents very good teachers and advisers at any time.

In conclusion, parents are not ideal teachers, and most children will generally need different teachers in their lives in order to have a more open view of the world. However, parents are generally the most committed of all teachers and make the greatest emotional investment in their children and their future.

Topic 9 书本知识与实践经验

You should spend about 40 minutes on this task.

Write about the following topic:

It has been said, "Not everything that is learned is contained in books." Compare and contrast knowledge gained from experience with knowledge gained from books. In your opinion, which source is more important?

Give reasons for your answer and include any relevant examples from your own knowledge or experience.

Write at least 250 words.

Sample Answer

People are always learning and practising through their whole lives. From reading words such as toy, car, train, etc. in the textbooks, people develop concepts and ideas. They further understand the actual meaning of these words by playing toys, and riding cars and trains, etc. Education (books) and experience are the two main channels for people to gain their knowledge. Each plays a different role for people. In my opinion, knowledge from experience is more important than that from books.

Firstly, experience can prove whether the knowledge from books is true or false. Textbooks are very wonderful in teaching people essential principles. What does the world look like? What is the basic law of change of people and things? We can learn a lot through primary school, secondary school until university. Nevertheless, people can only understand the real meanings of those things from books and justify them through practices. A few hundred years ago, people learned from textbooks that the earth was flat. Nevertheless, scientists found that it was wrong through observations and measurement.

Knowledge from experience can improve and advance the world and our society. As books have limitations, they only teach us about what people found in the past. The knowledge from the books is constrained to certain conditions and environment. The university courses only taught me very general things, but most knowledge I possess is obtained from dealing with various and complicated cases in my work.

There are a lot of new inventions and products, which could not be found in textbooks yet. Our society and world are developing through continuous practice. Some knowledge, never found in books, such as the Internet, e-business, etc., is all developed through new practice.

"The truth comes from practice and experience," goes an old saying. People are continually discovering new things and assessing the credibility of knowledge written in books. The knowledge from experience helps us much more than that from books.

Topic 10 学生必须上课

You should spend about 40 minutes on this task.

Write about the following topic:

Some people believe that university students should be required to attend classes. Others believe that going to classes should be optional for students. Which point of view do you agree with?

Give reasons for your answer and include any relevant examples from your own knowledge or experience.

Write at least 250 words.

Sample Answer

Some people may believe that going to classes should be optional, but I disagree. I don't think university students can expect to learn anything if they don't attend classes. Personal experience can help people learn about themselves and the world outside the classroom, but when it comes to learning academic subjects, students need to be in class.

In class they can learn a lot from teachers' elaborate instruction. To listen to teachers in class can do more than just to go over the material in textbooks after class. They draw their students into discussion on different topics. They present opposite points of view. They give students additional information, or show documentary films on the subject.

Also classes on any subject provide more than just facts. Students are taught how to learn, how to get information and then apply what they've learned to other situations. Their teachers are the best ones to help them with these skills. They cannot learn them just by reading textbooks.

By going to class, students can learn how to work with other members of the class. Often, students will be given group assignments. This is different from what they did in secondary school. Here they are with people from different backgrounds and experiences. In this situation, they learn how to cooperate with people different from themselves to achieve a common goal.

In short, students can get more than just information from teachers in class. They also learn how to learn, how to work with others, and how to work efficiently. These are not optional skills in life, so attending classes is optional.

Topic 11 学生的兼职工作

You should spend about 40 minutes on this task.

Write about the following topic:

In some countries, teenagers have jobs while they are still students. Do you think this is a good idea?

Give reasons for your answer and include any relevant examples from your own knowledge or experience.

Write at least 250 words.

Sample Answer

I don't think it is a good idea for teenagers to have jobs while they are still students. It can interfere with their studies, disrupt their home life, and take away part of their childhood that can never be replaced by anything else.

Education today is very complex and difficult. In order to 1earn and get good marks, a student must work very hard and concentrate on studies. This means attending classes from early in the morning until late in the afternoon, doing exercises, then going home and doing homework after school. It is a busy schedule for anyone. For those trying to hold a part-time job, it is even harder. Students need all their energy for their studies. If they are working after class at night, they will be tired the next day. They won't be able to concentrate. This will have a negative impact on their studies, and eventually on their academic performance.

Having a job can also disrupt a teenager's home life. Families spend less and less time together. If a teenager has a job to go to after school, he won't be home for dinner, and may not get home until late at night. This means he does not have much time to spend with his family. If he doesn't have a car, it can mean changes in his parents' schedules too. They have to drive him to work and pick him up.

The last but not the least drawback for a teenager to have a job while he is still a student is that he's missing out on the fun of being young. He has a whole lifetime in which he will have to earn a living. Being a student, he is not expected to work. It is also the last chance he can hang out with friends and just enjoy himself. Soon enough he will have to worry about paying the rent and buying food.

All in all, jobs bring money, but money is not everything. A teenager with a job gives up too much. No one should spend all his time on work, and especially a teenager.

Topic 12 人类活动与地球

You should spend about 40 minutes on this task.

Write about the following topic:

Some people believe that Earth is being harmed by human activities. Others feel that human activities make Earth a better place to live. What is your opinion?

Give reasons for your answer and include any relevant examples from your own knowledge or experience.

Write at least 250 words.

Sample Answer

The quality of human life has improved greatly over the past few centuries, but Earth is being harmed more and more severely by human activities. As we develop our technologies, we exploit more from our planet. Eventually, this will harm ourselves as well.

Our planet gives us everything we need, but natural resources are not endless. Strip mining devastates the whole regional environment, leaving bare and useless ground. Deforestation removes old trees that cannot be replaced. Too much fishing may reduce fish populations to the point where they cannot recover. We are too careless when taking what we want without giving anything back.

There are more people living longer than ever due to humans' development. So it is no wonder that Earth is bearing a much heavier burden. Anyone living in or near a city has experienced "urban sprawl". New shopping malls and apartments have appeared everywhere. Traffic gets worse and worse because roads cannot keep up with car growth. Keeping up with human's ever-increasing demands is hard enough. Environmental concerns come last in order to make economy develop fast enough. With economical growth comes pollution. Companies and communities dump waste into water. Landfills are full of trash. Emissions from factories pollute the air. Barrels of industrial waste and, worse, radioactive waste have made us feel nowhere safe to go. If we are not careful, we will destroy our planet.

People need to respect Earth and try to protect it. If we do not, what kind of future shall we have?

Topic 13 飞机是最重要的发明

You should spend about 40 minutes on this task.

Write about the following topic:

Nowadays the jet plane is considered to be one of the most important and influential inventions in the world. To what extent do you agree or disagree with this opinion?

Give reasons for your answer and include any relevant examples from your own knowledge or experience.

Write at least 250 words.

Sample Answer

I believe that one of the most important and influential inventions in the world should be the development of international jet transport. Since this type of transportation appeared in the 1950s, it has had some revolutionary effects. Because of the high speeds and the relatively low cost of this type of travel, it has changed the way people look at the world.

The most obviously important characteristic of jet travel is the high speed it enjoys. A hundred years ago, it took weeks to cross the Atlantic or Pacific Ocean by ship. Today, those trips can be completed in a matter of hours. One can attend a meeting in Paris and have dinner in New York the same day. These amazing speeds have changed people's concepts of space. Today the world is much "smaller" than it was in the past.

Another important aspect of jet travel is its relatively low cost. An international journey one hundred years ago was extremely expensive. Only wealthy people could afford to travel comfortably in first class. Poor people had to save for years to purchase a ticket, and the conditions in which they travelled were not very good. Today it is possible for more and more people in every country to travel in comfort. Thus it is possible for business people to do business all over the world, for students to attend universities in other countries, and for tourists to take vacations anywhere in the world.

In conclusion, the speed and low cost of international jet travel have changed the world. Nations are not as isolated as they were in the past, and people now think of the whole planet as they once thought of their own hometowns.

Topic 14 进步总是好的

You should spend about 40 minutes on this task.

Write about the following topic:

Do you agree or disagree that progress is always good?

Give reasons for your answer and include any relevant examples from your own knowledge or experience.

Write at least 250 words.

Sample Answer

Technology threatens and inflicts damage upon our quality of life. The scientific achievements of this century are creating widespread plagues that could soon destroy the entire world.

Let's take air for example. Due to massive air pollution, what we breathe is not safe as it used to be. Automobiles release exhaust fumes, and trucks and factories blow waste material into the atmosphere. After a period of time, atmospheric changes occur. The fumes that are collected in the atmosphere are slowly eating away the ozone layer. This layer of the atmosphere is what shields us from solar ultra-violet rays. Once this layer is gone, our natural protection against the sun would be gone, which would be a disaster for man.

Another plague of technology is nuclear power. The power that can energise entire cities with electricity could also be the power to destroy. After 1945, research on nuclear power has increased significantly. Contrary to the belief that it is safe, nuclear power is a threat to human beings. It is not like a fire that can be put out with water or carbon dioxide. Special equipments have to be used to deal with nuclear's damage. Afterwards, that place would remain radioactive for quite a long time, devoid of life and sound.

So you see, if technology development cannot be halted, our fate is sealed. Our end will not come about in a natural way, but due to our own technological achievements, life on Earth would cease to exist.

Topic 15 了解过去

You should spend about 40 minutes on this task.

Write about the following topic:

Learning about the past has no value for those of us living in the present. Do you agree or disagree?

Give reasons for your answer and include any relevant examples from your own knowledge or experience.

Write at least 250 words.

Sample Answer

People living in the present plan for and worry about the future. History, however, is the study of the past. Some people might say, "Given all the pressure from living in the present and worry about what is yet to come, why bother with what happened in the past? Given all the desirable and available branches of knowledge, why insist—as most American educational programmes do—on a bit of history? And why urge students to study even more history than they are required to?" Nevertheless, it's undeniable that learning about the past has its value. It will help us understand people and societies, and it will help us understand change and how the society we live in came into being.

History helps us understand people and societies. In the first place, history offers a storehouse of information about how people and societies behaved. Understanding the operations of people and societies is difficult, though a number of disciplines have been making the attempt. An exclusive reliance on current data would handicap our efforts. For example, how can we evaluate war if the nation is at peace—unless we use historical materials? How can we understand geniuses, the influence of technological innovation, or the role that beliefs play in shaping family life, if we don't use the experiences in the past? Consequently, history must serve, though imperfectly, as our laboratory, and data from the past must serve as our most vital evidence in the unavoidable quest to figure out why our species behaves this way in social settings. This, fundamentally, is why we cannot stay away from history: It offers the only extensive evidential base for the contemplation and analysis of how societies function, and people need to have some sense of how societies function to run their own lives.

History also helps us understand the social change and how the society we live in came into being. The second reason why history is inescapable follows closely on the first. The past leads to the present, and so to the future. Any time we try to know why something happened, we have to look for factors that took shape earlier. Sometimes fairly recent historical events will suffice to explain a new development, but often we need to look further back to identify the causes of change. Only through studying history can we grasp how things change. Only through history can we comprehend the factors that cause change; and only through history can we understand what elements of a society persists despite change.

In conclusion, I totally disagree with the argument that "Learning about the past has no value for those of us living in the present."

Topic 16 现代科技帮助学生学习

You should spend about 40 minutes on this task.

Write about the following topic:

With the help of technology, students nowadays can learn more information and learn it more quickly. Do you agree or disagree?

Give reasons for your answer and include any relevant examples from your own knowledge or experience.

Write at least 250 words.

Sample Answer

It is undeniable that continuously developing technologies have brought tremendous benefits, especially in learning. Learning has, in many ways, become easier than before. Take learning English for example. In the past, few students owned tape recorders, and learning materials were scarce as well. But today, tape recorders are getting more and more inexpensive, and diversified learning materials are readily available. On the other hand, new devices, such as MP3 or MD players, are available in market. And relevant learning materials (MP3 files) can easily and freely be downloaded from the Internet. However, it is a little bit hasty to assert that students can learn more information and learn it more quickly, simply because technology helps.

Technologies, as always, bring both benefits and detriments. For example, computers help students a lot in various ways, but at the same time have many negative, even harmful impacts on students. Most students nowadays play computer games, sitting before the table, staring at the screen and clicking the mouse button. The outcomes are cerebrum fatigue, visual deprivation and waste of time. Chatting on the Internet also wastes precious time. One of the side effects of too much dependence on keyboard is that students nowadays can seldom spell correctly. Worst of all, investigations have shown that more than half of the time that students have spent online was exhausted by browsing pornographic movies, pulp fictions or erotic photos and so on.

Students certainly want to learn more information and to learn more quickly. But technology itself is not the solution. Learning itself is a skill and it only develops in practice. Computers and other devices can certainly help, but they won't make study any less painful, and technologies, in fact, provide no solution to overcome indolence that everyone has. Learning has never been easy, and will not become easier merely because of technologies. It always requires tremendous effort and determination to learn something well. To exaggerate the fancy benefits of technologies will rather mislead than virtually help.

In conclusion, I totally disagree with the argument that with the help of technology, students nowadays can learn more information and learn it more quickly.

Topic 17 永不放弃

You should spend about 40 minutes on this task.

Write about the following topic:

The sentence "Never, never give up" means to keep trying and never stop working for your goals. Do you agree or disagree with the statement?

Give reasons for your answer and include any relevant examples from your own knowledge or experience.

Write at least 250 words.

Sample Answer

Near the end of the Second World War, Churchill delivered his famous and shortest speech: "Never, Never Give Up." The British, as well as people in many other countries, were tremendously encouraged, and finally went through the hardest period in human history.

Never to give up represents a strong and positive attitude towards life. Some people are ready to quit when they feel they cannot endure the difficulties of some work, or they don't think they can find a way to finish the required task. Such people usually become upset, disappointed by failure and lose their self-confidence, although they virtually can do everything well. In the case of acquiring a second language, most people fail simply because they have given up. Acquiring a second language might be the easiest task among diverse academic curricula, because one can be successful only by plain repetition, though it is painful and time-consuming.

Never give up. Such a strong belief often gives us a second chance. The fact that we failed somewhere does not mean we are going to fail everywhere, and it does not necessarily mean that we are deprived of opportunities to win. There is probably, if not always, a second chance. Many successful people did fail before. Yu Minhong, the founder of New Oriental School, was able to study in Peking University only after three attempts to pass the college entrance examination. He wasn't regarded successful after graduation. Among many things was the fact that almost all his classmates went abroad while he was, each and every time, refused by visa officers for unexplained reasons. Yet he never gave up, which led to his later success.

Psychology teaches us that we do get what we want, if we know exactly what we want and want the right thing. First of all, we must make sure that our defined goals are achievable, and that our carefully designed means are practical. A superficial claim like "I wanna be a millionaire!" brings nothing, and an unrealistic goal like "inventing a machine that will never comsume energy" is absolutely meaningless. But if we want to acquire a second language, it is both realistic and meaningful. By careful planning and persistence, we have no reason to fail. And numerous examples tell us that even if learning methods are imperfect, many people still can finally attain great achievements. Therefore, in most cases, "Never, never give up" is really something that we should always bear in mind.

Topic 18 男女分校

You should spend about 40 minutes on this task.

Write about the following topic:

Boys and girls should attend separate schools. Do you agree or disagree?

Give reasons for your answer and include any relevant examples from your own knowledge or experience.

Write at least 250 words.

Sample Answer

In some countries, people live in a culture where it is not appreciated for boys and girls to say love to each other. Moreover, it is absolutely shameful if such affairs happen on campus. To avoid this kind of allegations, some people assert that boys and girls should attend separate schools. I don't think it's a good idea.

Is there anything wrong when a little boy says "I love you" to a little girl? People in Hollywood movies often say "I love you" naturally to friends, family members, partners in work, even an unfamiliar taxi driver! But in reality, not surprisingly, many people have never said "I love you" to their parents, even seldom to their mates or children. "Love" in some cultures often carries subtle connotations related to immoral affairs. It doesn't seem a question whether there is anything wrong with it, but a question that there must be something wrong if a teenager dares to say anything about love!

Even if there must be something wrong when a teenager falls in love, is it something so appalling or evil that we adults have to prevent it or even fight against it? Have we ever discovered any prudent evidence which clearly proves it is really something bad? It is, in fact, quite natural that a little boy admires a beautiful girl or a little girl feels a smart boy appealing. And such emotions do not harm anyone: Alleged "premature love" is simply a nonexistent concept invented by ignorance. Girls and boys actually do not even know what love is! Perhaps they merely imitate the behaviour of adults around them. What we adults should do is not to make them believe "love" is evil, but to teach them what true love really means. Regrettably, those adults never realise that they actually fail to assume this responsibility, but presumptuously believe they are capable of eliminating love among boys and girls by separating them in different schools. It will never work.

Separate schooling was once a sign of discrimination of women, but today it reemerges to prevent "love affairs" among teenagers. A high school recently announced that it had already separated girls from boys in different classes. I can hardly imagine any benefit that such a scheme could produce except for further distortions of teenagers' nature.

Topic 19 童年最重要

You should spend about 40 minutes on this task.

Write about the following topic:

A person's childhood years (the time from birth to twelve years of age) are the most important years of a person's life. Do you agree or disagree?

Give reasons for your answer and include any relevant examples from your own knowledge or experience.

Write at least 250 words.

Sample Answer

It is generally accepted that a person's childhood years are very important years of their lives, but it is hardly appropriate to say those years are the most important in one's whole life.

We do not reject the importance of childhood years. Actually it is rather important for the later part of a person's life. Our lives, to a large extent, are subject to recognition of our surroundings. Our views about the world have been structured from the very early stage of our life, mainly through our daily experiences. Therefore, everyone actually sees the world differently from others. Though we all live in a single world, each and everyone of us, in fact, lives in distinctive worlds, which are determined by our distinctive perceptions that vary from individual to individual. Hence, we should not be surprised by the extent to which a person's life is influenced by one's childhood.

Childhood, however, is only part of one's life, and it is merely one of several factors that shape one's later life. Among various factors what is the most important is one's learning ability. Human beings are superior to any other animals on Earth simply because of their vigorous ability to learn. Psychology teaches us that training and self-training can dramatically change our characteristics and even the ability to learn, which may eventually change our lives. Furthermore, learning is a long process, which means every part of one's life could be an essential and crucial period, and could play an indispensable role in one's life. Examples are available everywhere. Einstein was considered as an idiot by his teacher when he was a child. Though the awkward attitude of his teacher made his childhood an awful one, Einstein did lead a wonderful life when he grew up.

Most parents, nowadays, seem to believe the statement that childhood is the most important phase of one's life, and therefore often force their children to learn those alleged essential skills for the sake of the future. The fact is that such behaviour is rather presumptuous, because there are still many other important factors that affect one's life.

Topic 20 动物园

You should spend about 40 minutes on this task.

Write about the following topic:

A zoo has no useful purpose. Do you agree or disagree?

Give reasons for your answer and include any relevant examples from your own knowledge or experience.

Write at least 250 words.

Sample Answer

Perhaps one of the most blameworthy factors that make some people frown at zoos and criticise that "A zoo has no useful purpose" is the high cost of maintaining them. However, it is too hasty to say so, since most zoos have their significance, both educational and scientific.

Modern zoos act as centres of education and are designed to help learning about animals an interesting and enjoyable experience. They provide visitors with the chance to see rare creatures, such as tigers, zebras, penguins and giant pandas, which come from many different parts of the globe. Zoos also introduce people to their local wildlife, offering a valuable learning experience in an increasingly urbanised world. At the same time, most zoos provide educational programmes to a wide range of ages. A visit to a zoo provides children with an opportunity to see animals other than household pets. For older school children, many zoos conduct classes or day trips that focus on different aspects of zoology and the impact of humans on animal life.

Modern zoos also have scientific importance and can function as a sanctuary for endangered animals, therefore helping maintain ecosystems. In zoos scientists can increase an animal population that can become self-sustaining in the wild. An example of a successful reintroduction to the wild is the père David's deer. This Asian deer was native to marshlands in northeast China before its habitat was destroyed more than 800 years ago, and it became extinct in the wild. Since then the species has been bred in zoos in China and later in Europe. In 1985 four père David's deer were released to the wild in an animal reserve in China, where they are now breeding successfully.

In conclusion, I totally disagree with the argument that a zoo has no useful purpose.

Topic 21 土地留给自然还是用于发展

You should spend about 40 minutes on this task.

Write about the following topic:

In your country, is there more need for land to be left in its natural condition or is there more need for land to be developed for housing and industry?

Give reasons for your answer and include any relevant examples from your own knowledge or experience.

Write at least 250 words.

Sample Answer

With a population accounting for about 20% of the world's population, China, my country, has been suffering from serious loss of arable land, which now hardly accounts for 7% of overall arable land of the world. Yet some people simply do not realise that land loss in China is so crucial that we, one day, might be incapable of averting catastrophe, if we close our eyes to it now.

After the entrance of the WTO, industry development is more and more important for our country. Yet industrial development without careful consideration regarding land preservation has caused problems more serious than people can ever imagine. We should be careful about the pollution which is inevitably caused by industrial production. Recent surveys have shown that pollution treatment engineering is not well financed in some factories in China, because attention is drawn to those much more obvious achievements. Industrial pollution accidents occur far more frequently in developing countries than in other more advanced countries. The urban waste also produces astoundingly large amount of pollution. Today the alleged "white pollution" is creeping all over the country—people throw plastic bags, and other plastic covers everywhere, never feeling anything is wrong.

It is no doubt that housing plays an important role in people's life. We must better people's housing conditions in order to improve their living standards. Therefore, housing building can be seen everywhere in China these years and a large quantity of arable land has been occupied by tall buildings. However, we should remember that we have to produce food for $1/5$ population of the world on the 7% arable land of the world. If the population continues to grow and the arable land continues to reduce, how can we achieve that goal?

To conclude, although we need land for housing and industry, it seems that we should try our best to leave as much land in its natural condition as possible. Otherwise, we will pay price in the future.

Topic 22 电视对孩子有害

You should spend about 40 minutes on this task.

Write about the following topic:

Television is bad for children. Do you agree or disagree?

Give reasons for your answer and include any relevant examples from your own knowledge or experience.

Write at least 250 words.

Sample Answer

By the time children go to school, they have spent one-third of their waking hours in front of the television. The enormous influence of TV is just beginning to be realised, and we have found out that most of its influences are bad. Far too much of a child's time is wasted. It is time for us to understand the bad effects that television can have on children.

One reason why watching TV is bad is that it induces kids to be potential consumers. They get surrounded by advertisements for dangerous toys, mindless games, and unhealthy foods. Children force their parents to buy them, for they themselves are not wise enough to detect the falsity of so much advertising.

Another bad effect of watching television is that kids are exposed to violence. They watch hours of murders, fights and crimes every week, without adults around to tell them that life is not like that most of the time. The effect of the heavy doses of violence to children, is that violence seems part of life, and that shooting and cheating are ways to succeed. Is that what parents want their children to learn?

Most serious of all, kids who often watch TV are becoming passive. They just sit back and let things happen without trying to do something actively. Children should be inventive; they have the ability to imagine a whole world of their own. But what happens when their imagination is not needed, when TV does all the imagination for them? Obviously, these kids are not going to grow up as inventive and imaginative as their parents, for they have been robbed of creative impulses by watching television.

Spending too much time watching TV is dangerous. It is time for parents to supervise their children's play, to engage in activities with their children, instead of putting them before the tube and hoping it will act as a baby sitter. The influences of TV are so serious that parents will have to be on their guard all the time in order to make sure that their children are not being harmed by being exposed to it.

Topic 23 年轻人与年长者

You should spend about 40 minutes on this task.

Write about the following topic:

There is nothing that young people can teach older people. Do you agree or disagree?

Give reasons for your answer and include any relevant examples from your own knowledge or experience.

Write at least 250 words.

Sample Answer

The older generation today always complains that many young people are unmotivated and directionless, that they lack aims and they will pay price for their behaviour in the future. Nonetheless, they don't realise youth are the products of their upbringing and the representation of their times. Thus, what they are and what they know will certainly be different from those of the older generation. Therefore, to say that the youngsters are useless is wrong, as they can also contribute in their own way, and teach the older generation a lesson or two.

As we all know, today's technology develops very fast. It is almost impossible for older people to keep up with every new technology that comes out. To young people, it is different; new things interest them. Furthermore, being young, they can absorb new knowledge like a sponge, much more quickly than the older generation does. Thus, they can help older people to get in tune with new technologies. Young kids, for example, can probably teach their grandparents to use the computer, which, in turn, will also be beneficial for their relationships.

In addition to this, by looking at the young people, we can learn about society better. As has been mentioned above, youngsters represent their times, hence, by understanding them, we can understand the development of society, as this group of age is the most outspoken. A good example would be the hippie movement in the US in the 1960s. The movement displayed their dissatisfaction with the social system, and their need for more freedom of expression of ideas.

As someone once said, "Life is a learning experience." From that, we can deduce that there is no stop to the process of learning. Instead of being critical of the youth, we should try to understand them and learn from them. After all, they are the future.

Topic 24 竞争与合作

You should spend about 40 minutes on this task.

Write about the following topic:

Some people say that the best preparation for life is learning to be cooperative. Others take the opposite view and say that learning to be competitive is the best preparation. Tell which one you agree with and explain why.

Give reasons for your answer and include any relevant examples from your own knowledge or experience.

Write at least 250 words.

Sample Answer

Learning to be competitive is clearly the best preparation for life. This becomes very clear as one has much experience in the world. Everyone has to make a living and must do everything they can to succeed. Let me explain.

In the first place, everyone knows that man is by nature a competitive, aggressive and selfish animal. Darwin, in *On the Origin of Species*, makes it very clear that the weak will die, and only the strong will survive. Since this is our fate, the only intelligent thing for us to do is to be strong, and to be a winner.

Also, in the business world, everyone knows that the most important work of the day is to beat your competitors. This can only be done by trying any possible means necessary to win, of course, legally. No one wants to go out of business, so you must compete. Also, you must be better than other employees you are working with, if you do not want to be fired.

Further, in the sports world, the strongest will come out as winners. They become our heroes and they are glorified in every way. In fact, the usual way our world rewards people is to give trophies to the winners, not to the losers. Everyone wants glory in life and learning to be competitive is the only path to it.

Therefore, the best way to survive in this world is to be competitive. However, learning to be cooperative is also necessary sometimes.

三、辩论型题目写法二：对称式写法

辩论型题目的另一种写法是对称式写法，与五段论式写法有所不同，介绍如下。

（一）结构

对称式写法的结构共分四段。

第一段：简略地说一下争议的问题，不要给出自己的观点。这和五段论式的写法完全不同。五段论式的写法，在开头段一定要旗帜鲜明地说出自己的观点。而对称式写法，只是说一下争论的话题，相当于五段论式写法开头段的引题部分。

第二段和第三段：两种观点各占一段，分别论述。第二段和第三段是文章的主要部分，因为两种观点各占一段，看起来是平衡的、对称的，所以这种写法叫做对称式写法。

第四段：给出自己的观点。

（二）第二段和第三段段落展开的方法

在对称式写法中，第二段和第三段的第一句话一般是一句总述。

接下来怎么展开有两种方法。第一种方法：如果能想出 2 – 3 个理由，每个理由写两句话左右。第二种方法：如果只能想出一个理由，那么与五段论式理由段的写法类似，把这段话的第一句总述当作是主题句，再写 6 句左右的支持句。

（三）第四段的写法

对称式写法是在最后一段说出自己的观点，既可以赞成其中的一个观点，也可以采取折中方案。所谓折中方案即认为双方观点都有优点，同时也都存在不足，应该取长补短，优势互补。

如果是赞成其中的一个观点，在说出自己的观点之后，应该再用几句话说明支持第二段或第三段中的观点的理由，这样可以强调突出自己的观点，避免给人论述不清的感觉。

下面，看一些用对称式写法写的雅思范文。其中第一篇范文给出了分析说明。

Topic 25 如何对待罪犯

You should spend about 40 minutes on this task.

Write about the following topic:

Should criminals be sent to prison or should they do something else as a punishment? Explain your opinion and give your reasons.

Give reasons for your answer and include any relevant examples from your own knowledge or experience.

Write at least 250 words.

Sample Answer

In recent years, a growing number of people have begun to challenge the existing practice of sending criminals to prison. They argue that the law offenders should be punished by doing something for the public. It is quite natural that people seldom reach a complete agreement on such a controversial issue.

Some people advocate that we should let criminals do something else as punishment. In the first place, they can get better reclamation this way. Doing something for society is a good measure, which not only punishes the criminals but also encourages them to begin a new life as well. Another reason is due to the limited jail space. Letting criminals do something outside jails decreases the cost of the government. Finally, the imprisonment of criminals cannot scare off possible criminals. Up to now, there is no evidence showing a direct link between the imprisonment of criminals and the decline of crime rate.

Some others approve of the imprisonment of criminals. First of all, it can ensure a safe living environment to the law-abiding citizens. For criminals like thieves, robbers, rapists or even murderers, it is improper or even dangerous to let them out of jails, because they still pose a threat to our society. Second, it is the best deterrent to those potential criminals. It will make would-be criminals think twice before they commit a crime. Last but not the least, it is a great spiritual consolation to victims. Those who suggest setting criminals free lay too much emphasis on the rights of criminals. They ignore the rights of victims.

Both of the above opinions make sense. After a careful consideration, I am in favour of the latter view that we should retain the practice of sending criminals to prison. It can guarantee the safety of citizens. It can reduce the crime rate. Furthermore, it serves as a punishment for the merciless offenders as well as a comfort to the innocent victims.

分析说明：

1. 结构

这是对称式结构，一共写了四段。

第一段：先引出题目，没有说出自己的观点。

第二段：给出一种观点，即让犯罪分子做一些其他的事情作为惩罚。第一句话是概述，然后陈述三个理由：犯罪分子可以得到更好的改造；节省监狱空间，降低政府的开支；囚禁犯罪分子根本不能降低犯罪率。每个理由都写了两句话左右。

第三段：给出另一种观点，即把犯罪分子关进监狱里。第一句话是概述，然后陈述了三个理由：保证公民的安全；震慑潜在的犯罪分子，降低犯罪率；安慰受害者。每个理由写了两句话左右。

第四段：说出自己的观点，即主张把犯罪分子关在监狱里。然后各用一句话重申第三段中的三个理由。

2. 高频词汇

challenge	/ˈtʃælɪndʒ/	*v.*	挑战
practice	/ˈpræktɪs/	*n.*	做法
punish	/ˈpʌnɪʃ/	*v.*	惩罚
natural	/ˈnætʃərəl/	*adj.*	自然的
seldom	/ˈseldəm/	*adv.*	不常，很少
reach a complete agreement			达成完全一致
punishment	/ˈpʌnɪʃmənt/	*n.*	惩罚
measure	/ˈmeʒə/	*n.*	措施
due to			由于
decrease	/dɪˈkriːs/	*v.*	降低
imprisonment	/ɪmˈprɪzənmənt/	*n.*	囚禁
evidence	/ˈevɪdəns/	*n.*	证据
decline	/dɪˈklaɪn/	*n.*	降低
crime rate			犯罪率
ensure	/ɪnˈʃʊə/	*v.*	保证

law-abiding citizen			遵纪守法的公民
criminal	/ ˈkrɪmɪnəl /	*n.*	犯罪分子
thief	/ θiːf /	*n.*	贼，小偷
robber	/ ˈrɒbə /	*n.*	抢劫犯
rapist	/ ˈreɪpɪst /	*n.*	强奸犯
murderer	/ ˈmɜːdərə /	*n.*	杀人犯
potential	/ pəˈtenʃəl /	*adj.*	潜在的
think twice			再思，再想
commit a crime			犯罪
spiritual consolation			精神安慰
victim	/ ˈvɪktɪm /	*n.*	受害者
make sense			有道理
consideration	/ kənˌsɪdəˈreɪʃən /	*n.*	考虑
in favour of			赞成
latter	/ ˈlætə /	*adj.*	后面的
guarantee	/ ˌgærənˈtiː /	*v.& n.*	保证
comfort	/ ˈkʌmfət /	*n.*	安慰
innocent	/ ˈɪnəsənt /	*adj.*	无辜的

3. 高分词汇

controversial	/ ˌkɒntrəˈvɜːʃəl /	*adj.*	有争议的
law offender			犯罪分子
reclamation	/ ˌrekləˈmeɪʃən /	*n.*	改造
scare off			吓唬住
improper	/ ɪmˈprɒpə /	*adj.*	不适当的
pose threat to			构成威胁
deterrent	/ dɪˈterənt /	*n.*	震慑
retain	/ rɪˈteɪn /	*v.*	保留
merciless	/ ˈmɜːsɪləs /	*adj.*	无情的

4. 高分句型

文章中高分句型很多，限于篇幅，只选择其中几句为大家分析一下。

（1）It is quite natural that people seldom reach a complete agreement on such a controversial issue.
在这样一个颇有争议的问题上，人们很少能达成完全一致，这是很自然的。

句型分析：

it 是形式主语，that people seldom reach a complete agreement on such a controversial issue 是主语从句，是真正的主语。reach a complete agreement on... 用得非常好。

（2）Doing something for society is a good measure, which not only punishes the criminals but also encourages them to begin a new life as well.
让他们为社会服务是个很好的措施，既对罪犯进行了惩罚，还能鼓励他们开始新的生活。

句型分析：

doing something for society 是动名词作主语，which not only punishes the criminals but also encourages them to begin a new life as well 是非限制性定语从句，not only...but also... 在定语从句中连接两个谓语部分。

（3）Up to now, there is no evidence showing a direct link between the imprisonment of criminals and the decline of crime rate.
到目前为止，没有任何证据表明在监禁罪犯和犯罪率的降低之间存在直接联系。

句型分析：

注意 there be 句型的使用。showing a direct link between the imprisonment of criminals and the decline of crime rate 是分词短语作 evidence 的后置定语。

（4）For criminals like thieves, robbers, rapists or even murderers, it is improper or even dangerous to let them out of jails, because they still pose a threat to our society.
像小偷、抢劫犯、强奸犯甚至杀人犯，释放他们是不合理甚至非常危险的，因为他们仍然对社会构成威胁。

句型分析：

for criminals like thieves, robbers, rapists or even murderers 是介词短语作状语。it 是形式主语，to let them out of jails 是动词不定式作真正的主语，because they still pose a threat to our society 是原因状语从句。pose a threat to our society 用得非常地道。

(5) Those who suggest setting criminals free lay too much emphasis on the rights of criminals.
那些赞成释放罪犯的人过分强调罪犯的权利。

句型分析：

those 是主语，who suggest setting criminals free 是主语的定语从句。lay too much emphasis on the rights of criminals 是谓语部分，这个短语用得非常好。

(6) After a careful consideration, I am in favour of the latter view that we should retain the practice of sending criminals to prison.
经过慎重的考虑，我倾向于后一种观点，即继续保留关押罪犯的做法。

句型分析：

after a careful consideration 是介词短语作状语，that we should retain the practice of sending criminals to prison 是同位语从句，说明 the latter view 的具体内容。

(7) Furthermore, it serves a punishment for the merciless offenders as well as a comfort to the innocent victims.
而且，这是对无情的罪犯的惩罚，是对无辜的受害者的安慰。

句型分析：

全句是并列宾语结构，it serves 是主语和谓语，两个宾语部分分别是 a punishment for the merciless offenders 和 a comfort to the innocent victims。全句不论结构还是用词都非常地道、准确。

Topic 26　学生评价老师

You should spend about 40 minutes on this task.

Write about the following topic:

Some people think that, in order to improve the quality of education, students should be encouraged to evaluate and criticise their teachers. Others feel that this will result in a loss of respect and discipline in the classroom. What do you think?

Give reasons for your answer and include any relevant examples from your own knowledge or experience.

Write at least 250 words.

Sample Answer

In many universities, students are encouraged to evaluate their teachers after each course. Some people believe the system has many advantages to both students and teachers. Others argue that it would lead to poor discipline in the classroom. Indeed, evaluation of teachers by their students has both pros and cons.

There are many drawbacks with student assessment. First of all, students are very young and, compared with their teachers, are less knowledgeable both in theory and practice on a subject. Therefore, they are unable to evaluate their teachers' performance in a sound way. Secondly, student assessment would lead to poor discipline in the classroom. If each student is allowed to decide on what, how and when to learn, class management would become impossible. Thirdly, in order to gain a better evaluation, teachers would seek to please each of their students by lowering requirements. This would do harm to students' academic performance in the long run.

However, advocates of student assessment have their reasons. Firstly, this kind of feedback can be used to improve teachers' performance. Teaching methods can only be successful if they are student-centred. Therefore, listening to students' constructive suggestions, teachers will have a better idea of what students' needs are and then are enabled to adjust their teaching to meet them. Secondly, evaluating will help students think on their own. Students should be encouraged to challenge their teachers' authority when necessary. Thirdly, the matter could be considered in a commercial way. Teachers are those who provide paid educational services while students, paying for their education, are customers. In this way, it can be fully justified that students have the right to evaluate the services they receive.

In my own opinion, student evaluations of teachers would be beneficial to both teachers and students. Firstly, teachers can adjust their teaching according to the information they obtain from the evaluation. Besides, students' ability of independent thinking and learning can be greatly improved. Moreover, the practice is the outcome of market economy. Students have the right to evaluate their teachers.

Topic 27 学习与实践

You should spend about 40 minutes on this task.

Write about the following topic:

Some people believe that the best way of learning about life is by listening to the advice of family and friends. Other people believe that the best way of learning about life is through personal experience. Compare the advantages of these two different ways of learning about life. Which do you think is preferable?

Give reasons for your answer and include any relevant examples from your own knowledge or experience.

Write at least 250 words.

Sample Answer

As we grow, we learn many things about life. Some of these lessons are easy and some are difficult. What is the best way to learn about life? Some believe that they can learn best by listening to the advice of others, while some other people believe that it is better to learn through personal experience. Both methods have their advantages.

In the first case, learning by listening to others, we have the benefit of learning from others' mistakes so as to avoid them ourselves. We can take advantage of the experience and wisdom of our friends and family. This will help us to make better decisions and avoid costly errors. Furthermore, the people who know us well can advise us effectively because they know our strengths and weaknesses. At the same time, they are, sometimes, able to see situations more objectively than we are.

In the second case, learning through doing, we have the advantage of gaining meaningful experience. We will no doubt better remember the lessons we learn by suffering the consequences caused by ourselves. Moreover, we can often develop other skills through personal experience and can learn from our mistakes. Finally, no two persons are exactly the same. Therefore, what family and friends think may be suitable for themselves, but not appropriate for us.

Given a choice between these two ways of learning about life, I would still choose the former, learning through the advice of others. This is because I believe I should take the advantage of all the resources available, and the experiences of my family and friends are a valuable resource. For example, if I were preparing to take my first trip abroad on my own, the advice of others who have already experienced such a trip could help me a lot. Just as we can learn from history, we can learn from the past of those close to us.

Topic 28 保留习俗与入乡随俗

You should spend about 40 minutes on this task.

Write about the following topic:

When people move to another country, some of them decide to follow the customs of the new country. Others prefer to keep their own customs. Compare these two choices. Which one do you prefer?

Give reasons for your answer and include any relevant examples from your own knowledge or experience.

Write at least 250 words.

Sample Answer

When people move to another country, they not only face a different environment and language, but also different customs. Every culture has its own customs, and all of them are valuable. However, deciding how to solve the problem of unfamiliar customs is a challenge for many immigrants. Some choose to follow the customs of the new country, while others prefer to adhere to their own customs. Each of these choices has some advantages as explained below.

When people choose to follow the customs of the other country, they may find that it helps them to adapt more quickly to the new society. They have something to discuss and share with their new neighbours, and sharing customs is one way for people to feel closer to one another. Thus, following the new customs may help immigrants feel more at home. It may also help them to see the positive things in the new environment and to forget their feelings of homesickness.

On the other hand, those who choose to continue following their own customs may also find that it helps them feel more at home. There are many things to adjust to in a new country and following their traditional customs may help people feel more comfortable in the new surroundings. More importantly, our customs are part of us. They are an expression of the culture that has shaped us. This is something that most of us would like to pass down to our children and share with others. Sharing our old customs can also bring us closer to our new neighbours.

To sum up, our customs have value and are an important part of our culture. Therefore, I don't believe that we should abandon our traditional customs when we move to another country. At the same time, I believe that we should learn about the customs of the new land we move to and follow those that appeal to us. In this way, we can remember and celebrate our old culture while adapting to the new one.

Topic 29　一小群朋友与一大群朋友

You should spend about 40 minutes on this task.

Write about the following topic:

Some people prefer to spend time with one or two close friends. Others choose to spend time with a large number of friends. Compare the advantages of each choice. Which of these two ways of spending time do you prefer?

Give reasons for your answer and include any relevant examples from your own knowledge or experience.

Write at least 250 words.

Sample Answer

Friends play a very important part in everyone's life. And each of our friends is special and unique. Some friends may be good advisors or confidants while others challenge our opinions or push us to try new things. Therefore, we may like to do different activities with different friends, and we may like to be with a large group of friends or spend time with just one or two. Each has its advantages.

One advantage of spending time with one or two close friends is that these friends usually know us well. We can communicate with them easily and are comfortable to share our feelings. We know that these good friends won't judge us. In addition, we are likely to share many of the same interests and will, therefore, find it easy to talk about many things. Finally, it is much easier to arrange activities when only two or three people are involved.

Spending time with large groups of friends also has its advantages. First, being with a wider variety of people exposes us to many more new ideas. We may be introduced to new things and develop new interests as a result. Also, we will more likely find someone to do things with when we associate with many friends. Last but not the least, being with a large group of people can be fun. There will always be enough people to play a game or make up a team.

As for me, although it can be fun to spend time with a large group of friends, I would prefer to stay with one or two close friends. It is easier for us to make our schedules and arrange a date to meet. Also, we have a deeper relationship, so I find the time that I spend with them very valuable. No matter how we like to spend time with friends, there is no doubt that friends are very important to us.

Topic 30 仔细计划与自由安排

You should spend about 40 minutes on this task.

Write about the following topic:

Some people prefer to plan activities for their free time very carefully. Others choose not to make any plans at all for their free time. Compare the benefits for planning free-time activities with the benefits of not making plans. Which do you prefer—planning or not planning for your leisure time?

Give reasons for your answer and include any relevant examples from your own knowledge or experience.

Write at least 250 words.

Sample Answer

In this busy society, our free time is very valuable to us. It is important that we take some time to relax and renew our energy in order to face the challenges ahead of us. Different people like to spend their leisure time in different ways. Some like to plan their activities so that they can make the most of their free time available while others prefer not to plan anything. In fact, both ways have their advantages.

When people carefully plan their leisure time, they will not waste any time on decision-making or last-minute preparations. This saves them time and, therefore, makes them feel that they have more free time to enjoy. Planning ahead also allows people to take advantage of the opportunity to participate in certain restricted activities. For example, by planning ahead, they can buy tickets for a concert or play that may later be sold out. Finally, being better prepared for an activity not only saves time but can make the outing more fun and more meaningful. It is not much fun to make a spontaneous trip to the beach only to find you have left your swimsuit at home.

However, unplanned leisure time also has its advantages. With no commitment to take part in a certain activity or meet a friend at a certain hour, the non-planner can take advantage of last-minute changes and opportunities. Furthermore, he would not be disappointed should his plans fall through, because he has made none. For example, if someone has looked forward to a baseball game all week, it is very disappointing if it is cancelled due to rain. Last but not the least, unplanned leisure time can be more relaxing. During the workweek, we must be punctual and face deadlines. Some people prefer to make their free time as different from that as possible.

Although both planned and unplanned leisure time have their benefits, I still prefer to plan my free-time activities. My free time is limited, and so I like to make the best use of it. By planning ahead, I can take part in the activities that I like and spend time with the people I want to see. And in case that my plans should be changed by unforeseen circumstances, I can always go to Plan B.

Topic 31 习惯与改变

You should spend about 40 minutes on this task.

Write about the following topic:

Some people enjoy change, and they look forward to new experiences. Others like their lives to stay the same, and they do not change their usual habits. Compare these two approaches to life. Which approach do you prefer? Explain why.

Give reasons for your answer and include any relevant examples from your own knowledge or experience.

Write at least 250 words.

Sample Answer

It has been said that man is largely a creature of habits. We all develop routines and habits in our everyday lives, whether we are aware of it or not. To some people, these routines are very important and even a small change, such as missing the morning paper, can affect their feelings all day. Other people dislike routines and change their habits often in order to ward off boredom. They may even go so far as to change their residence or job frequently. These two different approaches to life are extremes, but each has advantages and disadvantages.

In the first case, for people who dislike change, the dependence on routines and habits can provide a sense of security and convenience. Routines provide security because people do not have to wonder what will happen. In this rapidly changing world, it is sometimes reassuring to have a schedule to follow. Habits also make life more convenient because people do not have to think about what they must do next and do not need to worry about forgetting something. They can go through their daily routines automatically. However, this way of life is limiting when people are too dependent on their routines, because they may be upset when things do not go as expected. Moreover, they may miss many good opportunities to try new things.

In the second case, those people who seem to thrive on change are also reasonable. First of all, this kind of person is usually more open-minded to new ideas. He can, therefore, learn more and experience more. In addition, since he is not afraid to make changes in his life and take risks, he is more willing to take advantage of unexpected opportunities. This may lead him to a previously unforeseen success. But if a person is always seeking ways to change his life, he may not stick to things long enough to gain the most benefits from them. If he lacks the necessary determination and perseverance, it will be difficult for him to succeed by any means other than luck.

In my opinion, both of these lifestyles are extremes. Most people are not so dependent on their habits, nor are they addicted to changes. For me, a lifestyle somewhere between these two is ideal. I find some habits and routines comfortable and convenient, yet I am not afraid to face changes or take advantage of unforeseen chances to improve my life. Therefore, I will continue to follow my routine in daily life, but keep my eyes open for opportunities to change at the same time.

说明：

这篇范文在最后一段提出自己的观点，认为双方都有道理，应该取长补短，这也是可以的。

Topic 32 大学宿舍与校外公寓

You should spend about 40 minutes on this task.

Write about the following topic:

Students at universities often have a choice of places to live. They may choose to live in university dormitories, or they may choose to live in apartments in the community. Compare the advantages of living in university housing with the advantages of living in an apartment in the community. Where would you prefer to live?

Give reasons for your answer and include any relevant examples from your own knowledge or experience.

Write at least 250 words.

Sample Answer

At most universities there is a variety of housing options for students to choose from. Two of the most common ones are university dormitories and off-campus apartments. Each of these options has its advantages, and so students should make their decision carefully.

When considering moving into a university dormitory, students will find the following advantages. Firstly, it is usually located on campus and so it is very convenient for students to get to their classes, the library, and other university facilities. They will save the time that they otherwise spend commuting to campus. Secondly, living in a campus dormitory offers students a convenient life. They do not have to worry about cooking meals or paying utility bills on time because all these services are included. They will be able to devote more time to their studies and extracurricular activities. Finally, living in a dormitory makes it easy for students to meet others and develop friendships. In addition to sharing living and recreation space, students can meet others through activities organised by the university or the dormitory itself. This is especially helpful to new students.

As for off-campus apartments, there are also several advantages. First of all, living away from the university allows students to develop more independence. Taking more responsibility for their daily needs when they are students, they may find it easier to adjust to life on their own after graduation. In addition, the more independent lifestyle offers more freedom. Without university restrictions, students can arrange their own hours and set their own limits. Finally, students who live off-campus have more personal space. They do not have to share their bedrooms or bathrooms with many other people. This may allow them to better relax when coming back home.

In conclusion, both university dormitories and off-campus apartments offer certain advantages to students. Which one a student should choose depends on what is important to him or her. As for me, I would choose to live in a university dormitory for the first year. This would allow me to make friends and get accustomed to school life without the distraction of having to worry about my daily needs. Later, I would move into an off-campus apartment in order to develop my independence and enjoy a freer lifestyle.

说明：

这篇范文也是在最后一段提出自己的观点，认为双方都有道理，应该取长补短。

Topic 33 第一印象

You should spend about 40 minutes on this task.

Write about the following topic:

Some people trust their first impressions about a person's character because they believe these judgements are generally correct. Other people do not judge a person's character quickly because they believe first impressions are often wrong. Compare these two attitudes. Which attitude do you agree with?

Give reasons for your answer and include any relevant examples from your own knowledge or experience.

Write at least 250 words.

Sample Answer

When we first meet someone, we know nothing about his or her character. However, we often make some assumptions based on the first impression that the person makes upon us. Can these first impressions be trusted? Some people believe that our initial judgment of a person is usually correct, while others think it is often wrong. There are arguments to support both positions.

People who trust their first impressions believe that a person's appearance can be a good indication of not only his character, but also how he views himself and the people around him. It is true that we often send messages about our feelings without being aware of it. Body language is a good example of this. A person's postures, gestures and facial expressions can tell us a lot about what he is thinking and feeling. Furthermore, dressing and grooming can indicate whether someone cares enough about us so as to try hard to make a good impression.

On the other hand, first impressions can sometimes be misleading. People may be nervous with others they don't know well or in an unfamiliar situation. This may cause them to act in ways that do not reflect their true character. Likewise, some people may give a false impression because they may consciously or unconsciously fool the other person. In addition, one might simply be in a bad mood or not at his best for other reasons.

Considering the arguments above, I believe that it is better not to judge a person's character too quickly. First impressions are, at best, an indication of how a person is feeling at the moment, and may not indicate his or her true character. However, due to the importance that many people do place on the first impressions, we should be aware of the impression that we make on others. To sum up, I think we should not judge people according to the first impressions, but we should take care to make a good impression ourselves.

Topic 34 小城镇与大城市

You should spend about 40 minutes on this task.

Write about the following topic:

Some people prefer to live in a small town. Others prefer to live in a big city. Which place would you prefer to live in?

Give reasons for your answer and include any relevant examples from your own knowledge or experience.

Write at least 250 words.

Sample Answer

People seldom agree with each other, even to trivial issues such as preference between big cities and small towns. It's a little bit hasty to say that it is better to live in a big city than to live in a small town, or vice versa.

Living in a big city has several benefits. Firstly, there are more job opportunities readily available in big cities than in small towns. Furthermore, not merely are there more job positions in big cities, but the pay is more decent. Secondly, children are supposed to be able to receive an education of a higher quality compared with their counterparts who live in a small town. For most families, children's education is always put first. Finally, living in a big city has a superior living standard overall to that in a small town. There are more commodities and services in city markets; there are more public utilities available and people can even receive much more television channels in big cities.

However, living in a small town also has some advantages. People who live in a small town often have a much more comfortable lifestyle. Most of them are immune from the stress of heavy work. Although the average pay is much less than that of big cities, the price of daily necessities, such as vegetables or meat, is usually more inexpensive. Instead of suffering loneliness which is prevalent in big cities, children might grow up more happily and healthily because of harmonious neighbourhood in small towns. People in a small town do not have to get up so early in the morning because there are no traffic jams. They might have fewer television channels, but they have more friends readily available to chat or entertain with.

According to my current situation, although I am longing for the cozy atmosphere and relationship among neighbours and friends which almost only exist in small towns, I have chosen to live in one of the biggest cities in my country—Beijing, since I have had a pretty good job here, and decent pay. I think I would prefer living in a small town when I retire one day.

Topic 35 太空研究

You should spend about 40 minutes on this task.

Write about the following topic:

Some people believe that money spent on space research benefits all humanity. Others take the opposite view and say that money for this type of research is wasted. Discuss these two positions.

Give reasons for your answer and include any relevant examples from your own knowledge or experience.

Write at least 250 words.

Sample Answer

For over fifty years, a number of nations have been involved in the exploration of outer space. This research has been very costly, of course. Has this money been well-spent or wasted?

Some people believe that all or most space research should be cancelled because of its incredible expense, not only in terms of money, but also in terms of scientific and human resources. These people point out the fact that it cost billions of dollars to send astronauts to the moon, but all they brought back were some worthless rocks. These people say that the money and effort now being wasted in outer space could be spent on more important projects right here on Earth, such as providing housing for homeless people, improving the education system, saving the environment, and finding cures for diseases.

However, other people believe that space research has provided many benefits to humanity. They point out that hundreds of useful products, from personal computers to heart pacemakers to freeze-dried foods, are the direct or indirect results of space research. They say that weather and communications satellites, which are also products of space research, have benefited people all over the globe. In addition to these practical benefits, supporters of space research point to the scientific knowledge that has been acquired about the sun, the moon, the planets, and even our own Earth as a result of space research.

I agree with those people who support space research and hope it will continue. Space research, as shown, has already brought many benefits to humanity. Perhaps it will bring even more benefits in the future, which we cannot even imagine now. Moreover, just as individual people need challenges to make their lives more meaningful, I believe the human race itself needs challenges, and I think that the peaceful exploration of outer space provides a good one.

Topic 36 广告

You should spend about 40 minutes on this task.

Write about the following topic:

Some people say that advertising encourages us to buy things we really do not need. Others say that advertisement tell us about new products that may improve our lives. Which viewpoint do you agree with?

Give reasons for your answer and include any relevant examples from your own knowledge or experience.

Write at least 250 words.

Sample Answer

We, the TV generation, are more familiar with advertising than anything else. Advertising does play an important and positive role in our modern life, though it does have many disadvantages.

It is quite easy to find reasons for attacking advertising. Firstly, it is extremely costly to put an advertisement on TV or in newspapers. TV advertising, for instance, costs more than 100,000 yuan per minute during prime time. And this cost must eventually be paid by consumers. Secondly, it wastes valuable human resources: The advertising attracts and hires many talents in any country. In addition, from the social standpoint, advertising promotes products by famous images. For example, a brand named after a famous designer or a celebrity such as Li Ning, a former athlete in China, fascinates consumers by advertising to pay extra for the brand regardless of quality.

However, other people also argue in defence of advertising, for the sake of its economic function. In the first place, it has a valuable informative function, helping potential customers know about the characteristics and prices of products or where they can buy a particular product they need. Then, by stimulating demand for products, advertising creates jobs in manufacturing and service sectors. Finally, it can reduce prices by making mass-production possible.

As for my preference, I would like all advertising to be honest, amusing and informative. But if I must choose between living in a society with advertising and one without advertising, personally I prefer the former. China, for example, where advertising was not allowed in mass media before the 1980s, is now full of colourful lifestyles because of the advertisements in TV programmes and magazines.

至此，雅思写作考试辩论型题目的写法就讲完了，一共有两种写法：五段论式写法和对称式写法。下面，给出几个雅思写作考试的题目，每个题目提供两篇范文，Sample 1 用的是五段论式写法，Sample 2 用的是对称式写法，大家对照看一下。

Topic 37 考试

You should spend about 40 minutes on this task.

Write about the following topic:

Some people think that examinations have some bad effects on both students and teachers. Some people say they do a good job in the evaluation of students' performance. What is your opinion?

Give reasons for your answer and include any relevant examples from your own knowledge or experience.

Write at least 250 words.

Sample Answer 1

From primary schools to universities, students have to take many examinations. They even regard examinations as an indispensable part of their life. In most schools and colleges, examinations are used as a chief means of deciding whether a student succeeds or fails in a subject. However, although they work efficiently, the side effects are also enormous.

Examinations are unable to evaluate one's true ability. They can only test one's memory or the skills of working rapidly under pressure. Sometimes the future of a person may be decided by a single examination. How can one do his best when he is under the extreme pressure? In other words, it does not mean that all of those who get high scores in examinations possess great ability in practice. There are many stories that examination losers turn out to be great scientists or successful entrepreneurs.

Another effect is that examinations encourage bad study habits. Students tend to lay emphasis on the content which will be tested. They are encouraged to memorise rather than to think. Moreover, examinations induce cram during the exam week. However, after the examination, most children forget nearly all the information and facts they stuffed into their heads.

Examinations lower the standards of teaching as well. They deprive teachers of some freedom. Since teachers themselves are often judged by examination results, they have to spend much time training students for exam techniques instead of teaching as they expect. Furthermore, students are required to learn only what teachers tell them.

In conclusion, even though examinations have been used for a long time, they should no longer be used as the only means of evaluation. They cannot assess a student's overall abilities in learning and they have negative impacts on both students and teachers.

Sample Answer 2

In the long history of human education, great changes have taken place in every field of studies. However, testing a person by examinations is still regarded as the only reliable and feasible method to measure one's knowledge and ability. From primary schools to universities, students have to take various examinations. They even regard examinations as an indispensable part of their life.

Some people hold that examinations have negative impacts on both students and teachers. First of all, examinations are unable to evaluate one's true ability. They can only test one's memory or the skills of working rapidly under pressure. Secondly, examinations encourage bad study habits. Students tend to lay emphasis on what will be tested. They are encouraged to memorise rather than to think. Finally, examinations lower the standards of teaching. Teachers have to spend much time training students for exam techniques instead of teaching as they expect.

Many other people, however, believe examinations have some advantages. In the first place, they serve as a driving force to stimulate students to work hard. Laziness is part of human nature. Without examinations, students tend to ignore their studies. Moreover, the results of examinations are just like mirrors for both students and teachers. Students can assess themselves and teachers can adjust their teaching methods according to the information they obtain from examinations. Finally, till now no better methods have been discovered to replace examinations. Other forms of assessment are too time-consuming and therefore are infeasible.

In my opinion, examinations have positive effects on teaching. They make students work hard. They also provide a clear objective standard by which students can assess themselves and teachers can know what they should do next. Furthermore, at present no better methods are available. Therefore, I am sure examinations will continue to play an essential role in education.

Topic 38 相似朋友与不同朋友

You should spend about 40 minutes on this task.

Write about the following topic:

Some people like different friends. Others like similar friends. Which kind of friend do you prefer? Explain why.

Give reasons for your answer and include any relevant examples from your own knowledge or experience.

Write at least 250 words.

Sample Answer 1

Which kind of friend is more desirable, different friends or similar friends? Since people's criteria for friendship differ, they may never agree on the above issue. Personally, I have made friends with people from all walks of life, and these different friendships are such precious treasures of mine.

In the first place, a lot of friends can bring us many practical benefits. As the saying goes, "A friend in need is a friend indeed." Since we all need to move on in life, we need new friends to lead us to new adventures, new career opportunities and new life. In fact, most of us have to make new friends when we leave school and find employment. Besides, different friends can help us with different difficulties that we encounter in life. For example, a friend in a foreign country might be able to arrange cheap accommodation for us for a holiday.

In the second place, to contact with different friends gives a person a broad outlook to life. As the Chinese sage Confucius put it, "Where there are three men walking together, one of them is bound to be able to teach me something." Since we all have our weaknesses, the strengths of different friends can always complement each other. For example, from a friend who majors in computer science, I have learned how to design my own web page; by exchanging emails with an American pen friend, I have greatly improved my English writing ability. In addition, different friends can help me to enjoy a variety of interests, and we can always attract each other with our different hobbies, ideas and experiences. I feel that I can always learn something from my various different friends.

All in all, although "birds of a feather flock together", I would like to fly with "birds" of different feathers, which would certainly add colours to my life.

Sample Answer 2

Do you have many friends? Are they similar to you or different from you? Which kind of friend do you prefer?

Having friends whose character, hobbies and social status are similar to you can bring you many advantages. Maybe you are fond of collecting stamps, then what a pleasure it is to have a friend with the same taste, and exchange the little "treasures" with him; or maybe you are interested in playing tennis, then how wonderful it is to compete with your friend, also a big tennis fan, in a green field. Similar friends are easy to get along with, and between you and your friends, there is always something that all of you are familiar to. Because of the similarity, they can see something in the position of yours, and understand you better.

But how about making different friends? Yes, they may not have what you have, but they have what you don't have. Perhaps the least similar friends are Mr. Fogg, the protagonist in the scientific fiction *Around the World in Eighty Days*, and his ardent, humourous and talkative servant, Jean, who was not a bit like his old-fashioned master. But who can say that Mr. Fogg's courage and bravery during the great trip and his compassion towards Mrs. Aouda at the end of the story were not partly from the influence and help of Jean? A different friend is a mirror which can reflect your virtues and shortcomings. From him, you can find what you lack and learn what you need. When viewed from these perspectives, different friends may do more in shaping you than the similar ones do.

No matter how similar they are, every two friends have differences, and no matter how different they are, as friends, they have at least one similarity: the sincerity towards friendship. In the sincere friendship, you can find shelter from danger, courage in need, and hands willing to help. Open your heart to your friends, whether they are similar to or different from you, you may become the happiest person in the world.

Topic 39 警察佩带枪支

You should spend about 40 minutes on this task.

Write about the following topic:

Unlike other countries, the police in the UK do not carry guns. Some think this leaves citizens unprotected, while others consider it reduces the overall level of violence in society. What do you think?

Give reasons for your answer and include any relevant examples from your own knowledge or experience.

Write at least 250 words.

Sample Answer 1

It is reported that the police in the UK do not carry guns. I think the absence of guns is disadvantageous for the police in any nations. My opinion is based on the following reasons.

First of all, it's been a trend that violence is increasing in various parts of the world. More and more criminals, these days, carry guns and other dangerous weapons. If the police force only have pepper spray, batons and bulletproof vests for protection, it isn't enough to be a deterrent in today's society. The police should have proper equipment, i.e. a gun, so that they would hopefully not lose their lives and the local residents will feel safer and better protected.

However, some people think the police with guns may increase the overall violence in society, which means there'll be more gun-battles. In my opinion, gun carrying by the police should be regulated to ensure that police wouldn't hurt citizens except criminals. Firstly, the police should conceal weapons so as not to terrify ordinary people, for no one would like the feeling of seeing a police patrolling around with a big gun. Secondly, the police station should strictly regulate the usage of guns and the police who are negligent should be severely penalised. In this case, only in the most crucial circumstance, will the police be allowed to use guns to protect themselves and citizens. If all the police are very well trained for the gun using, citizens won't worry about that violence will be increasing. In addition, the government should also have rigid gun control regulations for the police.

For example, the police won't be issued excessive bullets; when they resign or retire, they have to turn back their guns; the police only carry guns when they are on duty, etc.

All in all, regulated gun-carrying by the police is necessary, which will be protective for themselves and other people as well. Furthermore, it'll improve the overall security of society.

Sample Answer 2

People in the UK, even the police, are not allowed to take guns. Some people argue that it may trigger off insecurity of city dwellers, whereas others assert that it can eliminate violence in society. Hereby, I would like to discuss both of these two perspectives in the following paragraphs.

Some people believe that the absence of guns is disadvantageous in many aspects in any nation. It has been a trend that violence is increasing in various parts of the world. More and more criminals, these days, carry guns and other dangerous weapons. If the police only have pepper spray, batons and bulletproof vests for protection, it is not enough of a deterrent in today's society. If the police have proper equipment, i.e. a gun, they would hopefully not lose their lives and the local residents will feel safer and better protected.

Others, however, hold the opinion that the police should not be allowed to carry guns. There have been plenty of cases that some robbers or thieves who committed crimes but did not deserve death were shot down by police. Further more, some unqualified and irresponsible policemen may hurt some innocent citizens, or even kill them when pursuing some culprits. Additionally, guns issued to the police may be lost, which will touch off an even worse situation. And thus, it will reduce the overall violence in our society if the police are not allowed to carry guns.

In conclusion, both sides of such a practice have their respective reasons and justifications. However, as people always expect a peaceful life, I personally agree with the latter view. If guns and other dangerous weapons are totally restricted in the modern world, violence and other relevant harmful behaviours will reduce. Hence, it is my sincere wish that governments of other countries would follow the example of the UK to avoid violence globally.

四、解释型题目的写法

解释型题目与辩论型题目有明显的区别。解释型题目是要求说明一种现象的原因、涉及的因素或解决的方法等。在雅思写作考试中，这种题目占 20% 左右。

解释型题目的写法分两种情况：

第一种情况：题目只有一个要求，如只要求说出原因、涉及因素或解决方法等。

例1：The 21st century has begun. What changes do you think this new century will bring?

例2：Groups or organisations are an important part of some people's lives. Why are groups or organisations important to people?

这种情况的写法，基本上与五段论式相同，一般写成四段或五段。

第一段：引出题目。

主体段落：写两段或三段。根据题目的要求，分别说出两个或三个原因、涉及因素或解决方法等，一个占一段。每段先写一句主题句，然后写若干支持句。

最后一段（可能是第四段也可能是第五段）：总结全文。

第二种情况：题目有两个要求，如要求说出原因，同时还要给出解决办法。

例1：It is generally acknowledged that families are now not as close as they used to be. Give possible reasons and your recommendations.

例2：What are the causes of water shortages? Please also offer some solutions to deal with this problem.

对于这种情况，有两种写法。第一种写法类似五段论式写法，写一个开头段，中间用两到三段回答第一个问题，最后用结尾段回答第二个问题。第二种写法类似对称式写法，写一个开头段，中间两段分别回答两个问题，最后写一个结尾段总结。

下面，看一些解释型题目的写作范文。

Topic 40 家庭成员关系不亲密

You should spend about 40 minutes on this task.

Write about the following topic:

It is generally acknowledged that families are now not as close as they used to be. Give possible reasons and your recommendations.

Give reasons for your answer and include any relevant examples from your own knowledge or experience.

Write at least 250 words.

Sample Answer 1

In the past, family was a very important concept in people's minds, and it was the centre of many people's lives. Nowadays, however, the relationship between family members is not as close as before. As far as I am concerned, it results from the following reasons.

The first reason is that people spend more time on their study and work. Compared with the past, people face fiercer competition and suffer from greater pressure. Therefore, they have to devote more time and energy to their careers. Some people are too occupied to spare time for their family. What is more, many jobs require people to work in other cities and many children have to leave their parents at an early age to study or work elsewhere. As time passes, these people become emotionally estranged from their parents.

Another reason is that there are more entertainments available. Nowadays high technology brings us more interesting things which can easily attract people's attention, such as watching TV, surfing the Internet or playing video games. As a result, people are indulged in these activities, totally neglecting the feelings of other family members.

To bring family members closer, people put forward various suggestions. Firstly, never bring your work home but leave it in your office. We should spare more time with family members no matter how occupied we are. Secondly, try to squeeze some time for a regular family dinner because dinner time is a perfect time and opportunity for people to exchange their feelings and ideas. Last but not the least, we should teach children the importance of family when they are still young.

说明：

这个题目有两个要求，既要说出原因，同时还要提出解决问题的建议。这篇范文的写法是类似五段论式写法。开头段，引出题目；中间两段回答第一个问题，说出了两个原因；最后一段给出了解决问题的建议。

Sample Answer 2

In the past, family was a very important concept in people's minds, and it was the centre of many people's lives. Nowadays, however, the relationship between family members is not as close as before.

There are several reasons for this phenomenon. The first reason is that people spend more time on their study and work. Compared with the past, people face fiercer competition and suffer from greater pressure. Therefore, they have to devote more time and energy to their careers. Some people are too occupied to spare time for their family. Another reason is that there are more entertainment forms available. Nowadays high technology brings us more interesting things which can easily attract people's attention, such as watching TV, surfing the Internet or playing video games. As a result, people are indulged in these activities, totally neglecting the feelings of the other family members.

To bring family members closer, people put forward various suggestions. Firstly, never bring your work home but leave it in your office. We should spare more time with family members no matter how occupied we are. Secondly, try to squeeze some time for a regular family dinner because dinner time is a perfect time and opportunity for people to exchange their feelings and ideas. Last but not the least, we should teach children the sense of family when they are still young and help them form some good habits like writing letters and making telephone calls to each other.

Family is the basic unit of society. It plays a significant role in our lives. In order to enjoy a harmonious family life and maintain a stable society, we should take efforts to build a close family relationship.

说明：

这篇范文的写法是类似对称式写法。开头段，引出题目；中间两段分别说出原因和给出解决问题的建议；最后一段总结全文。

Topic 41 城市存在的问题

You should spend about 40 minutes on this task.

Write about the following topic:

While people flood into big cities to seek jobs and happy life, there is a tendency for people to move out. What problems do big cities have?

Give reasons for your answer and include any relevant examples from your own knowledge or experience.

Write at least 250 words.

Sample Answer

Every year men and women crowd into cities in search of employment, decent living conditions, and the excitement and stimulation of urban life. According to a research, the population in Shanghai alone has increased 26% in the last three years. With the rise in urban population, many big cities have met various problems.

One big problem is the ever-increasing pressure caused by over-crowding. As more and more people flood into cities, city services and facilities have been strained to a breaking point. Cities have been exposed not only to the problem of traffic and housing, but to the problem of education, sanitation, employment and so on.

A second problem is the living environment. The rising of too many compacted high buildings strips people of sunlight, trees and grass—condemning them to live among stone and concrete, neon lights and endless traffic flows. Additionally, the growing number of cars and buses sends huge quantities of carbon dioxide into the atmosphere, making the air of cities unbreathable.

But of all the problems, the most serious and pressing one is the widespread crime, which is a threat to paralyse the city. Bank robberies which were unheard of in the past now occur more frequently. Not a single day passes without the reports of somebody being mugged, being kidnapped or being murdered, etc.

All these problems make big cities no longer attractive to people as years before. The tendency to move to the edge of the city or the suburban areas reflects this mentality. Unless there is some improvement, more and more people will seek to live in the suburbs.

Topic 42 水资源短缺

You should spend about 40 minutes on this task.

Write about the following topic:

What are the causes of water shortages? Please also offer some solutions to deal with this problem.

Give reasons for your answer and include any relevant examples from your own knowledge or experience.

Write at least 250 words.

Sample Answer

Since the beginning of time, water has been shaping the face of Earth. Water sustains human life, our environment and our cultures. But the global demand for water is increasing and the destruction of water-dependent ecosystems has accelerated.

From my point of view, the main reason of scarcity of water resource is the rapid population growth, especially in developing countries. In order to meet the great demand for water, people exploit water resource in various ways. Water supply sources are being stretched to their limits. And groundwater pollution is increasing rapidly. Research indicates that over 1 billion people still do not have access to safe water supplies and over 1.7 billion do not have access to adequate sanitation facilities.

Another reason is the development of industry and agriculture. In some developing countries, some private factories make use of water resource inefficiently and make much pollution. Irrigated farming also contributes to water scarcity. Despite the high yield, irrigation is extremely water intensive. It takes about 1,000 tons of water to grow one ton of grain and 2,000 tons to grow one ton of rice.

Finding solutions of the problem involves the increase of worldwide awareness and international cooperation. Every individual should realise water crisis and the necessity of water-saving. As to the government some effective measures should be taken, including erecting modern irrigation systems and increasing the number of sewage water recycling plants. Building more dams can also be an effective solution. Dams play an important role in detaining the surface rainwater flowing from mountains and would prevent the loss of rainwater straight into the sea.

Topic 43　21世纪会带来什么

You should spend about 40 minutes on this task.

Write about the following topic:

The 21st century has begun. What changes do you think this new century will bring?

Give reasons for your answer and include any relevant examples from your own knowledge or experience.

Write at least 250 words.

Sample Answer

Mankind has made great progress since scientific exploration began, and this progress seems to be accelerating. In the past hundred years we have seen inventions that have not only greatly improved our lives but changed the very way we live. There is no reason to believe that this rapid progress will not continue in the 21st century. Although there is no way to exactly predict what our scientists and entrepreneurs will come up with, there are indications that advances will be made in certain areas. The following are some examples.

Firstly, advances will continue to be made in the field of medicine that will allow people to live longer and healthier lives. In developed countries today most people already have a lifespan that was unusually long a hundred years ago. Steady progress has been made in the eradication of diseases and this should continue in the next 100 years. In addition, biotechnology in the field of genetics may someday allow us to develop bodies that are stronger and free of inherited defects. Perhaps we will even be able to clone ourselves. No matter what form these advances take, it is highly likely that we will greatly extend our lifespan in the new century.

Secondly, new technology has already brought people around the world closer. This trend will continue in the 21st century as communication becomes more efficient and affordable. Countries and their people have formed stronger bonds both economically and politically, such as the recent development of the European Union. Perhaps some day in the future national boundaries will disappear. However, one side effect of this globalisation is that many characteristics of individual cultures will be lost. Sadly, by the end of the century, some languages and art forms may only be found in museums.

Thirdly, we can expect both a growing population and demands for a higher standard of living to put increasing pressure on Earth's resources. We have already seen some of the effects of this pressure in the form of pollution and global warming. It is likely that these trends will also continue and that more damage to the environment will be done. On the other hand, perhaps we will find more efficient ways to make use of the available resources or develop alternative forms of energy. In that case, we may live with nature more harmoniously.

The scenarios above are just three of the many possible changes that this new century will bring. We can expect to see great advances in many fields, including medicine, communications, trade, transportation and production. Although there may be problems in the future, our ingenuity and inventiveness will help us to deal with them.

Topic 44 团体与组织的重要性

You should spend about 40 minutes on this task.

Write about the following topic:

Groups or organisations are an important part of some people's lives. Why are groups or organisations important to people?

Give reasons for your answer and include any relevant examples from your own knowledge or experience.

Write at least 250 words.

Sample Answer

Most people belong to at least one group or organisation. These groups or organisations include social clubs, special interest groups, sports teams, etc. Such groups or organisations play an important part in people's lives today because they provide both material and spiritual benefits.

Both formal and informal groups or organisations can provide their members with material benefits. For example, membership in an exercise class offers the benefit of improved health. In addition, groups or organisations which work towards a specific goal, such as passing legislation or improving a neighbourhood, help people to achieve that goal more efficiently by working together. Finally, some groups or organisations provide special benefits that are reserved for members, for example, a music or book club in which members receive special discounts.

Most groups or organisations also provide spiritual benefits, the most important of which is a sense of belonging. When people choose to join a group or organisation, the membership becomes part of their identity. In the group or organisation, they can find like-minded people and feel like part of a team. This gives the members both companionship and the opportunity to share their feelings with sympathetic listeners. Moreover, trying out different groups or organisations enables people to discover their interests and clarify their goals. Through this process they can find out where they best fit.

In conclusion, organisations or groups are important in our lives because they provide us with many advantages. They help us clarify our goals and interests and find the support we need to pursue them motivately and effectively. More importantly, they give us companionship and a sense of belonging.

Topic 45 我们这一代

You should spend about 40 minutes on this task.

Write about the following topic:

Every generation of people is different in important ways. How is your generation different from your parents' generation?

Give reasons for your answer and include any relevant examples from your own knowledge or experience.

Write at least 250 words.

Sample Answer

The world is constantly changing and so are the people in it. With each generation we see important developments that affect the ways they think and live their lives. Therefore, it is not surprising that each generation of people is different from the one before, and our generation is no exception. My peers and I differ from our parents in several important ways, including our views of the world and our expectations of the future.

People of my age usually have a more globalised outlook than their parents. Unlike the previous generation, we have been exposed to a wide variety of information about the world from a very early age. We have benefited from technological advances such as communications satellites and the Internet. These have truly made the world a global village and we have been greatly influenced as a result. We are not only concerned about our traditional way of life, but also about how life is led around the world.

Our expectations of the future are also different. This is mainly due to the greater prosperity and peace that we have enjoyed. Fewer of us have ever suffered true economic hardship and many of us have a good education and high standard of living. Although we are willing to work hard to succeed, we also value our leisure time. We are more likely to spend money on recreational activities than to save money for our old age in the future. Our social prosperity has made us more materialistic than our parents, also more carefree.

Given our different circumstances, it is not surprising that we are so different from the previous generation. Our parents may shake their heads and worry about these changes, but no doubt their parents did the same. Rather than to worry about what the next generation is coming to be, I believe it is smarter to discover and appreciate the advantages in these developments.

Topic 46 电影、电视影响人们的行为

You should spend about 40 minutes on this task.

Write about the following topic:

How do movies or television influence people's behaviour?

Give reasons for your answer and include any relevant examples from your own knowledge or experience.

Write at least 250 words.

Sample Answer

The impact that modern mass media have had on our daily life, and society in general, is undeniable. No doubt it will become even greater as the mass media continue to develop and as the relevant technologies become more and more sophisticated. The mass media will be so fascinating that, virtually, nobody will be able to escape. Already, it can be seen that western movies are exercising influence on our youthful generations: Some of them grow long hair regardless of their sex, commonly part of which is dyed golden; some wear jeans in each and every season, usually the knees of which are deliberately tattered; boys may be fond of earrings or other odd pendants, and girls may be keen on cigarettes and weird coarse language.

The major means by which the mass media influence the public is creating topics of discussion in society. The mass media offer people (consumers) issues to talk and think about. *Titanic* had enjoyed a worldwide popularity for its theme of extolling immortal love; *Prime Colour* and *Wag the Dog* met with national debates on the rights and duties of the President of the United States. Antiwar movies such as *Tears of the Sun* and *All Quiet on the Western Front* among numerous others have been raising many questions—Is any war really to uphold justice? Is it really worthwhile that an individual makes sacrifices to his country and at the same time ignores his own family or his personal values?

The mass media also shape our understanding of what is important, and what is not important. The "important" issues are usually to be found at the prime time of TV. The "unimportant" stories are usually the ones that are not being told at all. The "not very important" stories are probably very short and hidden in the late programmes. In fact, censorship is imposed on all mass media, including the Internet. By selecting public issues, the mass media make decisions for us. Even though there are critical individuals in any society, they are a definite minority; the public on the whole indeed lack critical thinking, and therefore they are often misled by the media.

In brief, the mass media, by offering topics and affecting the ways in which we discuss "the important issues", have a strong influence on our perception of the truth, of the world or of the structure of our society. We have to admit that it plays a role in our lives as a source of information, experiences, entertainment, amusement and relaxation.

Topic 47 人们寿命更长的原因

You should spend about 40 minutes on this task.

Write about the following topic:

In general, people are living longer now. Discuss the causes of this phenomenon.

Give reasons for your answer and include any relevant examples from your own knowledge or experience.

Write at least 250 words.

Sample Answer

People nowadays are living much longer than those in the past. In China, the average life expectancy has reportedly increased more than four years since 1990. Among various factors that contribute to this phenomenon are the continuously advancing food condition, the rapidly developing medical care system, and finally the current stable social and economic circumstances.

The food condition overall is becoming better and better, and is an important factor that makes people live much longer than before. First of all, foods are more hygienic. People today drink untainted mineral water, sterilised skim milk, which are cheaply supplied in supermarkets. Furthermore, foods are more nutritious, not to mention various carefully designed nutritious products. People can even ignore the possibility of being dystrophic because they can keep nutrients balanced by taking a pill of vitamin compounds every day.

Of equal importance is the rapidly developing national medical care system. Development of modern technology has always been amazing. Certain diseases such as tuberculosis, pneumonia and dysentery are now easy to remedy with low expense, while in the past they were all probably lethal. Dental technology seems to have developed little except its exorbitantly charged bill, yet the simplest technology contributes to people's longevity. It is not difficult to imagine that, if an individual who lived in the past got a toothache, without certain dental care which is common today, he was certainly in an awful situation: He might even die of a toothache!

Finally, the current stable social and economic circumstances are also a great influential factor. Social and economic circumstances have a dramatic effect on people's life expectancy. It was reported that Russian life expectancy dropped from 70 to 64 shortly after the disintegration of the Soviet Union. Apparently, people have less pressure in a more stable society, and the less pressure they suffer, the healthier they are. At the same time, various types of insurance are readily available, which make people feel safe and have, to a large extent, reduced people's anxieties, therefore, indirectly contributes significantly to people's longevity.

Topic 48 为什么上大学

You should spend about 40 minutes on this task.

Write about the following topic:

People attend college or university for many different reasons (for example, new experiences, career preparation, increased knowledge). Why do you think people attend college or university?

Give reasons for your answer and include any relevant examples from your own knowledge or experience.

Write at least 250 words.

Sample Answer

The college or university is a place where students can learn new and more knowledge and experience. Of course, different people have different reasons for studying in college or university. For example, some people want to study further after they graduate from college or university; some people hope to find a good job after graduation and also some people wish to change their present situation through studying in college or university. In my opinion, no matter what reasons people attend college or university for, studying is just a preparation for their future life.

First of all, students can gain new knowledge and experience from studying in college or university. There are many teachers and professors with abundant teaching experience, who teach students lots of new knowledge and help them to solve problems with their study. With their help, students can learn a lot of basic and specialised knowledge which is very helpful to their future work and study. After they finish their study in college or university, students can go to work in society and contribute in different fields.

Secondly, students can learn how to arrange their own time reasonably. Before their studying in college or university, their life may often be arranged by their parents, and their study by their teachers. It is very different for them to live and study in college or university, because students have to arrange their life and study by themselves. They now have the right to arrange their free time, such as when to get up, when to sport, when to finish the assignment, etc. This is very important experience for students' work and life in the future.

Thirdly, studying in college or university gives students the opportunity to live with other students and learn how to cooperate with other people. Usually, people feel uncomfortable about having to live with a stranger, because they do not know each other and perhaps their habits and personalities are different. But in the long run, it is good for them. They have to cooperate with each other and solve a lot of problems they will face together. Gradually, they can learn how to care for and understand other people. It is a preparation for students to go on to cooperate with other people in society.

All in all, students can not only gain lots of new knowledge from their books but also can learn much more necessary experience, such as how to arrange time and how to cooperate with other people. Therefore, studying in college or university is very important for their future work and life.

五、混合型题目的写法

混合型题目是指题目中有两个问题或要求，一个是辩论型的，一个是解释型的。在雅思写作考试中，这种题目占 10% 左右。

例1：In some countries, sports and entertainment personalities earn higher salaries than other professionals like doctors, nurses and teachers. Why do you think this happens in some societies and do you consider it is good or bad?

例2：In some countries, the national traditional arts are facing extinction. Some people think that the government should support them. Do you agree or disagree? What should the government do?

对于这种题型，处理的方法肯定是以辩论型的问题为主，保持五段论式或对称式的总体结构不变。另一个解释型的问题在开头段或结尾段中用两三句话回答就行了。

下面，看一些混合型题目的写作范文。

Topic 49 资助传统艺术

You should spend about 40 minutes on this task.

Write about the following topic:

Traditional arts civilised a nation. Do you think the government should subsidise musicians, artists, actors or drama companies? What should a government do?

Give reasons for your answer and include any relevant examples from your own knowledge or experience.

Write at least 250 words.

Sample Answer

Traditional arts, as valuable cultural heritage of a nation, are disappearing from the modern society. China, as one of the highly-civilised countries in the world, abounds in various forms of traditional arts, such as painting, calligraphy, music, architecture and drama, which are not only our national cultural treasures, but also a fortune of the world.

As the essence of a culture, traditional arts reflect a nation's artistic talents and traditions. Watercolour painting depicts a harmony between people and nature. Architecture illustrates a nation's aesthetic standards and religious belief. Cathedrals represent Christianity. Pagodas, totally different from cathedrals stylistically, are a symbol of Buddhism. Peking Opera enriches the history of the drama of our country.

However, traditional arts are leaving contemporary people further and further. One of the main reasons for this is that the local authorities aren't concerned enough and some art institutes lack funds and professionals, which are quite essential to the research and promotion of traditional culture. Another reason should be attributed to the impact of western cultures on traditions. For example, young people, especially youngsters, are addicted to western music like rock and roll, without any knowledge about traditional musical instruments. With the economic globalisation, traditional culture and arts will be in danger of assimilation.

Therefore, how to maintain and develop traditional arts should be one of the biggest concerns of the government. Firstly, the government should lay a fund for the research and promotion of traditional arts. Secondly, the art institutes and colleges should work out a long-term developing scheme, organising systematic research on traditional arts. Arts belong to a nation and the whole world as well.

The prosperity of traditional arts will diversify the cultures of the world.

说明：

这是一篇混合型题目的范文。题目中有两个问题，第一个是辩论型的，第二个是解释型的。本文以第一个问题为主，而第二个问题是在结尾段中处理的。

Topic 50 体育界和娱乐界人士的高薪

You should spend about 40 minutes on this task.

Write about the following topic:

In some countries, sports and entertainment personalities earn higher salaries than other professionals like doctors, nurses and teachers. Why do you think this happens in some societies and do you consider it is good or bad?

Give reasons for your answer and include any relevant examples from your own knowledge or experience.

Write at least 250 words.

Sample Answer

Nowadays, sports and entertainment personalities earn much higher salaries than other professional workers. As society progresses, people place great value on leisure and entertainment, and they spend more money on entertainment and sports, which is the main reason for those people to enjoy higher salary and popularity. In addition, the media and advertising industry give them great publicity which brings them even higher social status. However, in my opinion, too much attention placed on sports and entertainment personalities is not a good phenomenon.

Some other professional workers actually contribute more than sports and entertaining personalities. Teachers educate many individuals; perhaps through their influence, some students may change the destiny of mankind. Doctors save the lives of thousands of people. Physicists help people gain a better understanding of the nature, and perhaps contribute to the advancement of technology which is key to the progress of humanity. However, these professional workers might only receive $^1/_{10}$ or even $^1/_{100}$ of the money that sports or entertaining personalities obtain and only attract slight attention from the public.

If other professional workers earn higher salaries than sports and entertaining personalities, more young people can be motivated to choose scientific research as a career. Sports and entertaining programmes, on the other hand, are quite inadequate for people who want to meditate on and pursue deeper meanings of life.

The destiny of our children and ourselves is a concern that requires foresight. It is time that we should value the importance of all professional workers for the well-being of society.

说明：

这是一篇混合型题目的范文。题目中有两个问题，第一个是解释型的，第二个是辩论型的。本文以第二个问题为主，第一个问题是在开头段中处理的。

六、常用模板式句型

（一）在开头段引出题目

1. Admittedly, both sides are reasonable. But they are one-sided.
必须承认，双方意见都有道理，但它们都是片面的。
2. Admittedly, there are merits to both arguments.
必须承认，双方观点都有可取之处。
3. Advocates of ________ proclaim that ________.
赞成 ________ 的人声称 ________。
4. All these opinions make sense, and consequently it is hard to decide which one is more reasonable.
所有这些观点都有道理，因此，很难决定哪一个更合理。
5. Along with the development of society, more and more problems are brought to our attention, one of which is that ________.
随着社会的发展，越来越多的问题引起了我们的注意，其中一个问题就是 ________。
6. Along with the rapid development of society, remarkable changes have taken place in ________.
随着社会的快速发展，在 ________ 方面已经发生了显著的变化。
7. And a new problem has arisen: ________.
一个新的问题产生了：________。
8. ________ and ________ are two totally different ideas that have caused heated debate over a long period of time.
________ 和 ________ 是两个完全不同的观点。在很长一段时间里，它们引发了激烈的争论。

9. As a result, some people even suggest that ________.
因此，一些人甚至提出 ________。
10. As one of the most important inventions of the 20th century, ________ has a wide application in all aspects of our lives.
作为 20 世纪最重要的发明之一，________ 在我们生活的方方面面都有广泛的应用。
11. As society develops, people are attaching much importance to ________.
随着社会的发展，人们越来越重视 ________。
12. As the proverb goes: "Every coin has its two sides." ________ is no exception.
正像俗语所说，"每枚硬币有两面。" ________ 也不例外。
13. As the proverb goes: "So many people, so many minds." It is quite understandable that people from different backgrounds put different interpretations on the same issue.
就像俗语所说，"有多少人，就有多少观点。" 不同背景的人对同样的问题有不同的看法，这是可以理解的。
14. As society advances, people's demands have become increasingly diversified.
随着社会的发展，人们的需求变得多样化了。
15. As to how to ________, people put forward various suggestions.
关于怎样 ________，人们提出不同的建议。
16. As to whether it is a blessing or a curse, however, people take different attitudes.
然而，关于它是一件好事还是一件坏事，人们持不同的态度。
17. As to whether it is worthwhile ________, there is a long-running and controversial debate. It is quite natural that people from different backgrounds may have divergent attitudes towards it.
关于 ________ 是不是值得，长期以来一直存在争议。不同背景的人对它持不同的态度，这是很自然的。
18. As we know, ________ bring many benefits and conveniences to people.
正如我们所知道的，________ 给人们带来了很多好处和便利。
19. At present, some people think ________, while others claim ________. Both sides have their merits.
目前，一些人认为 ________，而另一些人声称 ________。双方都有道理。
20. Before giving my opinion, I think it is important to look at the arguments on both sides.
在提出我的观点之前，我认为看看辩论双方的观点是非常重要的。
21. Before rendering my opinion, I think it is important to take a glance at the arguments on both sides.
在说出我的观点之前，我认为先看一下双方的观点是很重要的。

22. Both patterns of ________ present advantages and disadvantages.
________ 的两种模式都各有优缺点。
23. Both sides of the argument have very strong feelings and sound reasons.
辩论双方的感情都很强烈，理由都很充分。
24. Both sides of the question are well supported by sound reasons.
问题的两方面都有很充分的理由支持。
25. But on the other hand, there are also many people who strongly advocate ________.
但是另一方面，还有很多人强烈赞成 ________。
26. But other people set forth a totally different argument about this case.
但其他人对此提出了一个完全不同的观点。
27. But others hold the view that ________.
但是其他人认为 ________。
28. But others, on the other hand, contend that ________.
但是另一方面，还有一些人主张 ________。
29. But people who advocate ________, on the other hand, argue that ________.
但是另一方面，赞成 ________ 的人认为 ________。
30. But people who are ________, on the other hand, maintain that ________.
但是另一方面，________ 的人坚持认为 ________。
31. But there are also people who are strongly opposed to ________.
但也有一些人强烈反对 ________。
32. Despite the advantages ________ has, some people claim we shall not lose sight of its adverse effects on ________.
有些人认为，尽管 ________ 有一些好处，但我们不应该忽视它对 ________ 的负面影响。
33. Everything has a good side and a bad side, and ________ is no exception.
任何事情都有好坏两方面，________ 也不例外。
34. Everything in the world has its own two sides. Without exception, ________ has both advantages and disadvantages.
世界上每件事情都有两个方面。毫无例外，________ 既有优点也有缺点。
35. For years, ________ has been seen as ________. But things are quite different now.
一直以来，________ 被认为是 ________。但是，现在情况大不一样了。
36. ________ has caused significant changes in family life and education. Some of these changes have been beneficial while others have been adverse.

________ 导致了家庭生活和教育的重大改变。一些改变非常有益，然而另一些改变却相反。

37. ________ has done many good things.

 ________ 已经做了很多好事。

38. However, as to whether it is a blessing or curse, there arises a heated debate among people with different backgrounds.

 然而，它究竟是一件好事还是一件坏事，这一问题在不同背景的人中引起了激烈的争论。

39. However, like anything else, ________ has more than one face.

 然而，像其他事情一样，________ 也有多面性。

40. However, recently this phenomenon has triggered a heated discussion as to whether ________.

 然而，最近这个现象引起了关于是否 ________ 的激烈讨论。

41. However, some others argue that ________.

 然而，一些人争辩说 ________。

42. However, there are a large number of people who hold a different view concerning this case.

 然而，关于这件事，很多人持不同的观点。

43. However, there are also some others who contend that ________.

 然而，也有一些人主张 ________。

44. However, there is a good side and a bad side to everything. ________ is no exception.

 然而，任何事物都有两面性。________ 也不例外。

45. However, views on this issue vary from person to person.

 然而，不同的人对这个问题有不同的观点。

46. However, with the advance of human civilisation, there is an increasing number of people who have raised doubts about whether ________.

 然而，随着人类文明的进步，怀疑是否 ________ 的人越来越多。

47. I strongly suggest that effective steps be taken as soon as possible to protect the community from the adverse impacts of ________.

 我强烈建议尽快采取有效步骤保护社区不受 ________ 的负面影响。

48. In a modern society, people have the freedom to choose ________ or ________. Although they normally coexist peacefully, they deserve some close examination.

 在现代社会，人们有选择 ________ 或 ________ 的自由。虽然他们一般会和平共处，但是还是值得仔细地思考。

49. In my mind, the following factors need to be taken into consideration.

我认为，必须考虑下列因素。

50. In order to minimise the negative effects described above, people set forth different solutions and here I would explore only two key ways.

为了减小上述的负面影响，人们提出不同的解决方法。在这里，我将只探讨其中主要的两种。

51. In recent years, an increasing number of people have begun to challenge against the existing practice of ________. They argue that ________.

最近几年，越来越多的人开始怀疑现行 ________ 的做法。他们认为 ________。

52. In recent years, there is a growing number of people who ________.

近年来，________ 的人越来越多。

53. In the process of modern urban development, we often find ourselves in a dilemma.

在现代城市的发展中，我们经常发现自己处于进退两难的境地。

54. In these days, the issue of whether ________ has aroused people's discussion.

近来，关于是否 ________ 的问题引起了人们的讨论。

55. Inevitably, on the other side, there are others who strongly advocate the practice of ________.

另一方面，不可避免地，还有一些人强烈赞成 ________ 的做法。

56. ________ is rapidly gaining its popularity all over the country.

________ 在全国很快流行开来。

57. It becomes so widespread that people cannot help asking: ________?

它变得那么普遍，人们不禁要问：________?

58. It has caused a heated public debate among us.

它在我们中间已经引起了激烈的、公开的辩论。

59. It has long been regarded as a beneficial practice to ________. However, in recent years, some people have been raising doubts about this practice.

________ 一直被认为是一个好的做法。然而近年来，有人对此做法提出了质疑。

60. It is not easy to render the reasons for this complicated phenomenon which involves several factors.

要给这个牵涉到几个因素的复杂的现象作出解释不是一件容易的事情。

61. It is often difficult for people to decide whether to choose ________ or ________.

选择 ________ 还是选择 ________ 对人们来说通常是困难的。

62. It is often the case that ________.

通常情况是 ________。

63. It is quite natural that people seldom reach a total agreement on such a long-running controversy.
人们对这样一个长期有争议的问题不能达成一致的看法，这是很自然的。
64. It is so crucial that we cannot afford to make a single mistake. However, it is not always easy to make a prudent satisfying choice. Sometimes we find ourselves involved in dilemmas.
它是如此的重要，以至于我们不能出一点差错。然而，作出一个谨慎而又令人满意的选择不是很容易的。有时我们发现自己处于进退两难的境地。
65. It would inevitably evoke a strong repercussion among people from different walks of life.
它不可避免地会引起各界人士的强烈反响。
66. Just as the saying goes: "No garden is without weeds." ________ has both advantages and disadvantages.
常言道："没有无杂草的花园。" ________ 有优点也有缺点。
67. ________, just like anything else in the world, has its bright side and dark side.
像世界上其他事物一样，________ 有积极的一面也有消极的一面。
68. Many people have the idea that ________. However, many others disagree that ________. Both sides of the question of whether ________ are supported by good reasons.
很多人认为 ________。然而，其他人不同意 ________。关于是否 ________ 这个问题两方面的理由都很充分。
69. Many people would claim that ________.
很多人声称 ________。
70. Nevertheless, people seldom reach an absolute consensus on such a controversial issue.
然而，在这样一个有争议的问题上，人们很少达成绝对的一致。
71. Nothing in the world is perfect, so is the ________.
世界上没有完美的事物，________ 也一样。
72. Now we are entering a brand-new era full of opportunities and innovations, and great changes have taken place in people's attitude towards some traditional practices.
现在我们正在进入一个充满机遇和革新的新时代，人们对一些传统做法的态度产生了很大的变化。
73. Now we are entering a new era, full of new knowledge and innovative ideas.
现在我们正在进入一个充满了新的知识和思想的新时代。
74. Nowadays, more and more people agree that ________.
现在，越来越多的人同意 ________。
75. Nowadays, some may hold the opinion that ________. But others have a negative attitude.

现在，一些人持有 ________ 的观点。但是另一些人则持有相反的态度。

76. Nowhere in the world has the issue of ________ been so much debated as in our society.
世界上没有哪个地方像我们这样对 ________ 的问题有如此之多的争论。

77. Nowhere in the world has the issue of ________ been more popular than ________.
世界上没有任何地方关于 ________ 的问题比 ________ 更普遍。

78. Of course, ________ also has advantages to some extent.
当然，________ 在某种程度上也有优点。

79. Of course, ________ also have some negative effects.
当然，________ 也有一些负面的影响。

80. On such a controversial issue, people seldom reach an absolute consensus.
在这样一个有争议的问题上，人们很少达成绝对的一致。

81. On the contrary, the advocates also advance cogent arguments in defence of the system.
相反，赞成者提出了有利的证据来维护这个做法。

82. On the other hand, ________ also have some negative effects.
另一方面，________ 也有负面影响。

83. On the other hand, some other people strongly despise the above attitude.
另一方面，一些人强烈鄙视上面的态度。

84. On the other hand, there are also many opponents who strongly disagree that ________.
另一方面，有许多反对者强烈反对 ________。

85. One of the difficult questions that today many people are facing is whether to choose ________ or ________. More and more, ________ is seen as the main method in ________ (doing something). Yet there are some people who cast serious doubts on ________.
今天很多人正面临的一个难题，是选择 ________ 还是 ________。________ 越来越被看作是（完成某事） ________ 的一个主要方法。但是也有一些人很是怀疑 ________。

86. Other people's opinion is just the opposite. They strongly believe that ________.
其他人的观点正好相反，他们坚持认为 ________。

87. People have different ideas about it.
人们对它有不同的看法。

88. People may prefer one to another, although some have no opinion about it.
虽然一些人没有什么观点，但人们可能会喜欢一个，不喜欢另一个。

89. People who support ________ give some or all of the following reasons.
支持 ________ 的人给出以下几个或全部的理由。

90. People, who advocate that ________, have their sound reasons.
赞成 ________ 的人有他们的道理。

91. People's views, however, are divergent on the matter in question. Some people are of the opinion that ________.
然而人们对这个问题的看法是不同的。一些人认为 ________。

92. ________ plays such an important role that it undeniably becomes one of the biggest concerns of today's world. There arises a question: Is it a blessing or a curse?
________ 起到这样重要的作用，不可避免地成为当今世界最受关注的问题之一。这样就出现问题了：它是一件好事还是一件坏事呢？

93. Recently the issue of whether or not ________ has been in the limelight and has aroused wide concern in the public.
最近，是否 ________ 的问题已经成为焦点，引起了公众广泛的关注。

94. Recently the phenomenon has aroused wide concern. Some people are in alarm that ________.
最近，这个现象引起了广泛的关注。一些人担心 ________。

95. Recently there arises a heated debate over whether it is wise to ________. People's views, however, are divergent on the matter in question.
最近，关于 ________ 是否明智引起了激烈的争论。人们在这个问题上的观点各不相同。

96. Recently, the issue of ________ has been brought into public focus.
最近，________ 这个问题引起了公众的关注。

97. Recently, there is a heated debate as to whether ________.
最近，对是否 ________ 进行了热烈的争论。

98. Recently, there is a heated debate on the issue of ________.
最近，关于 ________ 有一场激烈的争论。

99. Recently, this phenomenon has aroused wide concern and heated public debate has arisen.
最近，这种现象引起了广泛的关注并激起了热烈的讨论。

100. Recently, this phenomenon has been brought to public attention with people standing on two different sides.
近来，这个现象引起了公众的关注，人们持两种不同的观点。

101. Regarding these reasons, I think there are some ways to ________.
考虑到这些原因，我认为有许多方式去 ________。

102. Some people advocate that ________.

一些人赞成 ________。

103. Some people are of the opinion that ________.

一些人认为 ________。

104. Some people believe ________ because (of) ________. These people point out the fact that ________. They also argue that ________. However, other people stand on a very different ground. They believe that ________. They firmly point out that ________.

一些人认为 ________ 因为 ________。这些人指出 ________ 这一事实。他们还认为 ________。然而，另外一些人站在完全不同的立场上。他们相信 ________。他们坚定地指出 ________。

105. Some people believe that ________. Other people take the view that ________.

一些人相信 ________。另外一些人认为 ________。

106. Some people contend that ________ has proved to bring many advantages.

一些人认为 ________ 已经被证明带来了很多益处。

107. Some people deem it is a dangerous signal and call for public awareness of the negative effects it has brought about. Some even put forward a proposal that ________.

一些人说它是一个危险的信号，要公众警觉它所带来的负面影响。一些人甚至提出建议：________。

108. Some people even put forward the idea that ________.

一些人甚至提出 ________。

109. Some people examine this issue from another angle.

一些人从另一个角度来审视这个问题。

110. Some people hold the opinion that ________ is superior to ________ in many ways. Others, however, think quite differently on the question of ________.

一些人认为 ________ 在很多方面都优于 ________。然而，其他人在 ________ 的问题上的看法截然不同。

111. Some people say that ________, other people suggest that ________.

一些人认为 ________，另外一些人建议 ________。

112. Some people think ________. Others, however, believe ________. Which you prefer depends on your own experience, lifestyle and emotional concern.

一些人认为 ________，但是，另一些人相信 ________。你更喜欢哪一个取决于你的经历、生活方式和情感因素。

113. Some people welcome it with applause. They claim it is a good idea.

一些人极力赞成这个观点。他们断言这是一个好的想法。

114. Some say ________, but others take a negative attitude.
一些人认为 ________，但其余的人持相反的态度。

115. Thanks to China's policy of reform and opening-up, there has been earth-shaking economic and social progress in the past two decades and people's living standard has improved, but at the same time it gives rise to a host of serious social problems like ________.
随着中国改革开放政策的实施，在过去的 20 年中，经济和社会都取得了巨大的进步，人们的生活水平提高了。但与此同时，也产生了一些严重的社会问题，像 ________。

116. That is a very important thing for people nowadays.
那对现在的人而言是一件非常重要的事情。

117. The case is not rare. It has now drawn increasing attention to the plight of ________.
这种情况并不罕见，现在已经引起了公众对 ________ 的困境越来越多的关注。

118. The causes may be inner and outer influences.
原因可能是内部的和外部的影响。

119. The controversial issue is often brought into public focus. People from different backgrounds hold different attitudes towards the issue.
这个有争议的问题经常引起公众的关注。社会各界人士对这个问题有不同的态度。

120. The dilemma is whether it is better to ________.
问题是 ________ 是不是更好。

121. The discussion about whether or not ________ is a very controversial one.
关于是否 ________ 的讨论是非常有争议的。

122. The discussion as to whether the ________ is a blessing or a curse arouses most people's interests.
关于 ________ 是一件好事还是一件坏事的讨论引起了大多数人的兴趣。

123. The following suggestions should be taken into consideration when we are seeking solutions to ________.
当我们寻找 ________ 的解决方案时，必须考虑下列建议。

124. The human race has entered a completely new stage in its history. With rapid economic globalisation and urbanisation, more problems are brought to our attention.
人类已经进入了历史上一个全新的时代。随着经济快速地全球化和城市化，更多的问题引起了我们的关注。

125. The incident is not isolated. It has now drawn much attention to the issue of ________.
这一事件不是孤立的。它现在引起了公众对 ________ 问题的关注。

126. The issue whether it is good or not to ________ has aroused a heated discussion all over the country.
关于 ________ 是好是坏的问题在全国引起了热烈的讨论。

127. The opponents argue that ________.
反对者认为 ________。

128. The phenomenon has aroused wide concern among people.
这个现象已经引起了人们广泛的关注。

129. The story is not rare. It has now drawn public attention to the problem of ________.
这种情况并不少见。它现在引起了公众对 ________ 问题的关注。

130. The title statement is the focus these days and any speech about it would surely strike the top lines of most newspapers.
这个问题是近期的焦点，关于它的任何说法都会成为大部分报纸的头版头条。

131. There are a number of reasons for ________.
________ 的出现有多种原因。

132. There are different views concerning this topic.
关于这个话题，有不同的看法。

133. There are people on both sides of the argument who have very strong feelings.
争论的双方都有一些人的感情很强烈。

134. There are several reasons for this phenomenon.
这种现象的出现有许多原因。

135. There are several reasons for this problem.
这个问题的出现有几个方面的原因。

136. There are several reasons which suggest that ________.
有几个原因说明 ________。

137. There are several reasons why ________.
有几个原因说明为什么 ________。

138. There are some people who voice serious doubts about ________.
有一些人很怀疑 ________。

139. There arises a heated debate as to whether we should ________.
我们是否应该 ________ 引起了热烈的讨论。

140. There arises a very controversial issue to whether we should ________.
我们是否应该 ________ 是一个有争议的问题。

141. There is a general discussion today on the issue of ________. Those who criticise

________ argue that ________. They believe that ________.

今天，关于 ________ 有一场广泛的争论。批评 ________ 的人认为 ________。他们相信________。

142. There is a good side and a bad side to everything. It goes without saying that ________.

任何事物都有好坏两方面。不用说 ________。

143. There is a heated debate over ________.

关于 ________ 有激烈的争论。

144. There is a long-running controversy as to whether ________, of which people have quite different opinions.

关于 ________ 是一个长期有争议的问题，人们持有大不相同的观点。

145. There is a public controversy nowadays over the issue of ________. Those who criticise ________ argue that ________. They believe that ________, but people who favour ________, on the other hand, argue that ________.

今天，关于 ________ 有着普遍的争议。批评 ________ 的人认为 ________。他们相信________。但是另一方面，赞成 ________ 的人却认为 ________。

146. There is a public debate today about the problem of ________. Those who object to ________ argue that ________. They believe that ________.

今天，关于 ________ 有着公开的讨论。反对 ________ 的人认为 ________。他们相信________。

147. There is much discussion nowadays as to the problem of ________. Those who object ________ argue that ________. They believe that ________, but people who advocate ________, on the other hand, argue that ________.

今天，关于 ________ 的问题有很多的讨论。反对 ________ 的人认为 ________。他们相信 ________。但是另一方面，赞成 ________ 的人却认为 ________。

148. There is no denying that everything has more than one face and ________ is no exception.

不能否认，任何事物都有多面性，________ 也不例外。

149. There is no denying that there is some truth in the above point of view.

不可否认，上述观点有一定的道理。

150. There is probably a little bit of truth in both arguments and the opinions stated by both sides make sense and consequently, it is hard to choose the better one of them.

两种观点都有些道理，双方的意见都有理，因此很难从中选出更好的一个。

151. There will often spring up a heated discussion as to ________. A sizable percentage of the people like to ________.

关于 ________ 通常激起激烈的讨论。相当比例的人喜欢 ________。

152. They often fall into two big groups, one for it and the other against it.
他们经常一分为二，一方赞成，一方反对。

153. This controversy describes the dilemma faced by many people.
这一争议反映了很多人面临的难题。

154. This has aroused a heated debate among citizens. Some people welcome the programme with applause; others strongly oppose it.
这在市民中引起了激烈的争论。一些人热烈赞成这个项目，而另外一些人却强烈反对。

155. This is a controversial issue, which often arouses heated discussions among people.
这是一个有争议的问题，经常引起人们热烈的讨论。

156. This is a very controversial issue and people hold quite different opinions of it.
这是一个很有争议的问题，人们持有截然不同的观点。

157. This issue is so controversial that people can hardly reach an absolute consensus.
这个问题争议性太大，人们很难达成绝对的一致。

158. This issue should be well taken into consideration.
这个问题应该仔细考虑。

159. This phenomenon also poses us a prominent social problem: ________.
这个现象给我们提出了一个突出的社会问题：________。

160. This problem is a much debated one in that it affects everybody in their daily lives.
这个问题有很多人在讨论，因为它影响了每个人的日常生活。

161. This question is a very controversial one.
这是一个很有争议的问题。

162. Those people who approve of the practice of ________ hold that ________.
赞成 ________ 做法的人认为 ________。

163. Those people who are strongly against the practice assert that ________.
那些强烈反对这种做法的人认为 ________。

164. Those people who strongly approve of ________ have cogent reasons for it.
强烈赞成 ________ 的人有强有力的理由。

165. Those who argue for ________ say that ________.
那些赞成 ________ 的人说 ________。

166. Those who criticise it argue that ________.
批评它的人认为 ________。

167. Those who have already benefited from practising it sing high praise of it.

从这个做法中受益的人们对此歌功颂德。

168. Those who oppose it argue that ________.

反对它的人认为 ________。

169. To agree or disagree with it is a matter of balancing between its pros and cons.

同意还是反对它，是一个在它的优点和缺点之间取得平衡的问题。

170. To choose ________ or ________ is something of a dilemma to the public.

选择 ________ 还是 ________ 对公众来说是一件很棘手的事。

171. To my mind, this is one of the side effects brought about by this modern world.

在我看来，这是现代社会带来的一个副作用。

172. Towards the same issue, many others advocate that ________.

对同样的问题，还有很多人认为 ________。

173. Undeniably, there are points on both sides of the argument.

不可否认，争论的双方都有道理。

174. ________ undoubtedly plays an increasingly significant role in modern life.

毫无疑问，________ 在现代生活中起到了日益重要的作用。

175. Until recently, ________ was viewed as ________. But nowadays people are taking a fresh look at it.

直到最近，________还被认为是________。但是，人们现在以新的眼光来看待它了。

176. Upon to the question that which is better, ________ or ________, people have different opinions about it. ________ has its advantages, but at the mean time, it has many disadvantages, too.

关于 ________ 和 ________ 哪一个更好的问题，人们持不同的观点。________ 有它的益处，但同时，它也有很多弊端。

177. We always face the circumstances: ________ or ________. There are advantages and disadvantages on both sides.

我们总是面临这样的情况：________ 或 ________。两方面各有优缺点。

178. We cannot deny that we have benefited a lot from ________.

我们不能否认我们已经从 ________ 中受益匪浅。

179. When asked ________, some people think ________ is more desirable while some prefer ________.

当被问到 ________时，一些人认为 ________更好，然而一些人则喜欢 ________。

180. When asked about ________, the vast majority of people say that ________, but other people view ________ as ________.

当被问到 ________ 时，绝大多数的人认为 ________，但其余的人把 ________ 看作 ________。

181. When faced with ________, quite a few people claim that ________, but other people think of ________ as ________.

当面临 ________ 时，相当一部分人认为 ________，但另一些人把 ________ 看作 ________。

182. When it comes to ________, most people tend to believe ________. But others consider ________.

当说起 ________ 时，大多数人相信 ________，但是另一些人认为 ________。

183. When it comes to ________, the majority of people think that ________, but other people conceive ________.

当涉及到 ________，大多数人认为 ________，但另一些人则认为 ________。

184. When it comes to ________, most people believe that ________, but other people regard ________ as ________.

当涉及到 ________，大多数人认为 ________，但其余的人把 ________ 看作 ________。

185. Whether ________ is a very controversial question. There are people on both sides of the argument who have very strong feelings.

是否 ________ 是一个很有争议的问题。双方的态度都很强硬。

186. While the rhythm of people's life is speeding up, a lot of changes have taken place in people's daily habits. ________ is mushrooming everywhere.

随着人们生活节奏的加快，人们的日常习惯发生了很多变化。________ 在各处快速增长。

187. With the development of society, people's ideas about ________ have changed dramatically.

随着社会的发展，人们关于 ________ 的观念发生了极大的变化。

188. With the development of society, ________ is becoming increasingly important.

随着社会的发展，________ 越来越重要。

189. With the rapid development of science and technology, ________.

随着科学技术的快速发展，________。

190. With the remarkable development of human civilisation, people enjoy better living standards and the quality of citizens has improved greatly.

随着人类文明的巨大发展，人们的生活改善了，公民的素质也大大提高了。

191. With the steady economic growth in the country, people's living standard has greatly improved, the rhythm of people's life is speeding up and a lot of changes have taken place in their daily life.
随着国家经济的稳步增长，人们的生活水平大大地提高了，人们的生活节奏日益加快，日常生活发生了很多变化。

192. Yet when it comes to ________, people from different backgrounds hold different attitudes.
然而，当说到 ________ 时，不同背景的人持有不同的观点。

（二）说出自己的观点

1. A close inspection of these arguments would reveal how flimsy they are.
仔细审查这些观点将会看出它们是多么浅薄。

2. A close scrutiny of these arguments would reveal how fallacious they are.
对这些争论进行详尽的研究后，可以看出它们是多么的荒谬。

3. According to my personality and fondness, I would prefer ________ rather than ________.
根据我的个性和喜好，我倾向于 ________ 而不是 ________。

4. After a thorough consideration, for my part, I am in favour of the latter view that ________.
经过周密的考虑，我赞成后一种观点：________。

5. After pondering this question on many occasions, I finally reached the opinion that ________ is something worthy to do and I cannot skip it.
在反复考虑这个问题后，我最后得出这样的结论，________ 值得去做，我不会放弃它。

6. After pondering this question on many occasions, I have finally reached the conclusion that ________ is something I truly want to do and is worthwhile.
在反复考虑这个问题后，我最后得出一个结论，________ 是我真正想做的，而且也值得去做。

7. Again, I would state my objection to this issue again after analysing the following three reasons.
在分析下面三个原因后，我愿意再次提出对这一问题的反对意见。

8. Although ________ possesses potential advantages over ________, it cannot be compared with ________ in more concrete advantages.
虽然 ________ 拥有的潜在优势超过 ________，但在很多具体的优点上却无法和 ________ 相比。

9. Although at first glance these arguments sound reasonable and appealing, they are not borne out by a careful consideration.
虽然乍看上去，这些论据似乎是合理的和吸引人的，但它们都经不起仔细的推敲。
10. Although I appreciate that ________, I cannot agree with the agreement.
虽然我欣赏 ________，但我不同意这个协议。
11. Although it is an admirable idea, ________ is not always a realistic option.
虽然这是一个好主意，________ 却是一个不切实际的选择。
12. Although many people believe that ________, I doubt whether the argument bears much analysis.
虽然许多人相信 ________，但我怀疑这个观点是否经得起分析。
13. Anyway, I agree with the idea of ________.
不管怎么说，我同意 ________。
14. As far as I am concerned, I agree that ________.
就我来说，我同意 ________。
15. As far as I am concerned, I am inclined to be on the side of the latter view.
我的观点更倾向于后者。
16. As far as I am concerned, I have a preference for ________ over ________.
就我来说，我更偏向 ________ 而不是 ________。
17. As far as I am concerned, it is advisable ________.
我认为更明智的是 ________。
18. As far as I am concerned, its advantages outweigh its disadvantages.
我的观点是，它的利大于弊。
19. As far as I am concerned, this proposal seems a bit absurd and ridiculous.
在我看来，这个提议有点荒谬可笑。
20. As for me, ________ is preferable in many ways.
对我来说，________ 有很多可取之处。
21. At first thought, it may seem to be an attractive idea, but it does not bear closer analysis when we find ________.
乍一想，这似乎是一个很吸引人的想法，但当我们发现 ________ 时，它就经不起进一步的分析了。
22. At first thought, the idea seems to be a sound and attractive one, but carefully weighing in mind, I can hardly consent to this proposal because it is so inconceivable and impractical.
猛然一想，这个主意似乎是合理的和吸引人的，但仔细考虑之后，我不能同意这个提议，因为它难以让人相信，不切实际。

23. At first thought, this opinion seems to be sensible and sound. But at the second thought, I find that it is not often the case.
猛然一想，这个意见似乎合情合理，但再一想，我发现并不总是这样。

24. At first thought, it may seem to be an attractive idea, but it doesn't bear closer analysis.
乍一想，这个主意似乎很不错，但它却经不起更深入的分析。

25. At the risk of addressing the issue too directly, the advantage of ________ always outweighs that of ________.
坦率地说，________ 的优势比 ________ 强。

26. At the risk of sounding too direct, I prefer to ________.
恕我直言，我更倾向于 ________。

27. But after careful consideration of the above reasons, I, personally, stand on the side of the advocates.
经过仔细考虑上述原因后，我支持正方。

28. But I can hardly share this point of view.
但我很难支持这个观点。

29. But I cannot share this point of view for several reasons.
但因为多种原因我不同意这个观点。

30. But I think it is unadvisable to ________.
但我认为 ________ 是不明智的。

31. But I would have to say that, if I were faced with the decision, I would probably follow the contemporary trend and choose ________.
但是我要说，如果我面临这个抉择，我愿意跟随当代的潮流选择 ________。

32. But if I am concerned, I can only disagree with the above view and the reasons are given below.
但是如果问我，我不同意上述观点，原因如下。

33. But if one has considered the following perspectives, he could only agree with the argument as I do.
但是如果一个人考虑到下面的几个方面，他就只能像我一样，同意这个观点。

34. But its bright side should not keep us from its dark side.
但它的优点不能掩盖它的缺点。

35. But whatever the advantages of ________, I like ________.
但不论 ________ 有多少优点，我还是喜欢 ________。

36. But when we consider these two sides more carefully, we can see that the harm outweighs the

merits.

但当我们更加仔细地考虑这两方面的因素后，我们能够看出弊大于利。

37. Carefully weighing in mind, we easily find how fallacious they are.

仔细考虑后，我们很容易发现它们是多么荒谬。

38. Certainly, I am aware of the fact that both methods have potential pitfalls, nevertheless, from my point of view, I vote for ________.

确实，我意识到两种方式都有潜在的危险，不过，在我看来，我选择 ________。

39. Considering the social atmosphere today, it is not a time to choose ________. It is high time to choose ________.

考虑到今天的社会环境，选择 ________ 不是时候，而是选择 ________ 的大好时机。

40. Contrary to the generally accepted ideas, I would like to prove that ________.

与被普遍接受的观点相反，我想证明 ________。

41. Deep down, I disagree with the above statement, and support the superiority of ________.

实际上，我不同意上面的观点，而支持 ________ 的优越性。

42. Despite its good intentions, I think ________ doesn't make sense.

虽然出发点是好的，但我想 ________ 没有道理。

43. Despite its merits, it also brings some problems to solve.

尽管它有很多优点，也带来一些需要解决的问题。

44. Despite the advantages ________ has, it has its disadvantages.

尽管 ________ 有优点，也存在许多不足。

45. Despite the advantages advocated by some people, I am totally against this view.

尽管这些优点得到一些人的赞同，但我完全反对这个观点。

46. Despite the fact most people like ________, I would like to choose to ________.

尽管许多人都喜欢 ________，我个人却选择 ________。

47. Despite the fact that ________ enjoys considerable advantage of ________, it cannot be compared with ________ in several main aspects.

尽管 ________ 在 ________ 方面有相当大的优势，但在很多主要的方面却不能和 ________ 相比。

48. Despite the fact that ________ has a unique advantage over ________, it cannot compete with ________ in many cases.

尽管 ________ 有 ________ 所没有的独特优势，但在很多方面却不能和 ________ 相比。

49. Despite the fact that most people prefer ________, I would like to choose ________ because

of the following reasons.

尽管许多人更喜欢 ________，我还是选择 ________，原因如下。

50. Despite the fact that the majority hold the opinion ________, I doubt whether the argument can bear much analysis.

尽管许多人拥护 ________，但我仍然怀疑这个论点是否经得起推敲。

51. For my part, I stand on the latter opinion that ________.

站在我的立场上，我支持后一种意见：________。

52. From my part, I completely agree with the latter.

从我这方面看，我完全同意后者。

53. From my point of view, I vote for the latter one.

以我的观点，我选择后者。

54. From my point of view, it is more advisable to choose ________ than to choose ________.

依我的看法，选择 ________ 比选择 ________ 更好。

55. From my point of view, it is more advisable to choose ________ rather than ________.

在我看来，选择 ________ 比选择 ________ 更可取。

56. From the reasons presented above, I think the pros outweigh the cons.

根据上述理由，我认为其优势超过了弊端。

57. Generally, I prefer to ________.

通常，我更喜欢 ________。

58. However, along with the positive effects, they have resulted in new social problems.

但是，伴随着积极的影响，它们还引发了新的社会问题。

59. However, although many people prefer ________, I feel that it is better to ________.

然而，虽然很多人偏爱 ________，我感觉 ________ 更好。

60. However, despite of the popularity of ________, its impacts on people are often negative.

然而，不管 ________ 多么流行，它对人们的影响仍是负面的。

61. However, I do not think that this view can hold water.

然而，我不认为这个观点站得住脚。

62. However, if I have to choose one of these two, I am in favour of the latter opinion that ________.

但是，如果我必须从两者中选择其一，我倾向于后一种观点：________。

63. However, in my opinion, I prefer the idea that ________.

但是，我的观点是 ________。

64. However, just as a coin has two sides, ________ has its demerits.

但是，正如每枚硬币都有两面，________ 也有它的缺点。

65. However logical and valid the arguments may be, they only skim the surface of the issue.
不管这些争论显得多么有逻辑性和有道理，它们仅触及到了问题的表面现象。

66. I believe that the argument is valid.
我认为这个观点是有根据的。

67. I can hardly share the proposal that ________.
我很难同意 ________ 的提议。

68. I completely disagree with this statement that choosing ________ has more advantages than choosing ________.
我完全不同意选择 ________ 比选择 ________ 有更多益处这一观点。

69. I do strongly support the idea that ________.
我强烈支持 ________ 的观点。

70. I feel such an attitude is negative, and that it can only bring further misfortune.
我感觉这种态度是消极的，只会带来更大的不幸。

71. I find the statement of ________ is too narrow.
我发现对 ________ 的论述太狭隘。

72. I fully agree with the statement that ________.
我完全同意 ________ 的观点。

73. I fully support the statement above.
我完全支持以上的观点。

74. I side with the former view that ________.
我同意前一个观点：________。

75. I totally agree with this statement, and I will explain why it is the case.
我完全同意上述观点，我愿意解释为什么。

76. If asked to make a decision, I would prefer ________.
如果要求我作出决定，我更愿意 ________。

77. If I were forced to agree with one of the two methods, my choice would be ________.
如果硬要我从两种方法中选择其一，我的选择是 ________。

78. If it is up to me to make a choice between ________ and ________, I would rather choose ________ over ________.
若要我在 ________ 和 ________ 之间作出选择，我宁愿选择 ________。

79. In my opinion, ________ is as important as, if not more than, ________.
我的观点是，即使 ________ 不比 ________ 更重要，起码二者也同等重要。

80. In my opinion, I argue that ________.
在我看来，我认为 ________。
81. In my opinion, it is more advisable to ________ than to ________.
我的意见是，________ 比 ________ 更明智。
82. In my opinion, the advantages of ________ are more than those of ________.
我认为，________ 的好处比 ________ 的多。
83. In my part, I prefer ________ rather than ________.
依我看，我更倾向于 ________ 而不是 ________。
84. In my part, I would like to vote for ________.
以我的观点，我支持 ________。
85. In my point of view, I like ________ much more than ________.
在我看来，我喜欢 ________ 比 ________ 多得多。
86. In spite of all the claims of ________, I doubt the value of ________.
不管人们对 ________ 怎样断言，我仍然怀疑 ________ 的价值。
87. In spite of disadvantages of the system, we cannot pay no heed to the fact that it brings us more advantages.
不管这个体系多么不好，我们不能忽略这一事实：它给我们带来更多的是好处。
88. In the discussion, many people suggest that ________, but I argue that ________。
在讨论中，许多人建议 ________，但我认为 ________。
89. Many people advocate that ________. They claim that ________. My opinion is the same as theirs for the following reasons.
许多人支持 ________。他们声称 ________。我的看法同这些人一样，原因如下。
90. My view is that ________.
我的看法是 ________。
91. No belief is so undesirable as the one that ________.
没有一个观点像 ________ 那样令人不快。
92. No doubt, I prefer ________, since there are too many benefits that outnumber its disadvantages. But ________, on the other hand, has advantages no more than its disadvantages.
毫无疑问，我选择 ________，因为它的优点比它的缺点多。而 ________ 则弊大于利。
93. No idea is more untrue now than the one that ________.
现在，没有比 ________ 更不可信的观点。
94. No issue is more important now than the one that ________.

现在，没有比 ________ 更重要的问题。

95. No opinion is so foolish now as the one that ________.

现在，没有像 ________ 一样愚蠢的观点。

96. No view is more dangerous now than the one that ________.

现在，没有比 ________ 更危险的观点。

97. Nonetheless, pound for pound, I reckon that ________ is more advantageous.

然而，综合权衡，我认为 ________ 更有利。

98. Now, it is commonly believed that ________; such people think ________, but I wonder whether ________.

现在，大多数人相信 ________，这些人认为 ________，但我怀疑是否 ________。

99. Now, it is generally accepted that ________; its advocators believe ________. But I wonder ________.

现在，被广泛接受的观点是 ________，支持者认为 ________；但我怀疑 ________。

100. Now, it is increasingly acknowledged that ________; its advocators think ________, but I doubt whether ________.

现在，被广泛接受的观点是 ________，这一观点的支持者认为 ________，但我怀疑是否 ________。

101. Now, it is widely held that ________; its advocators think ________, but I wonder whether ________.

现在，大多数人相信 ________，支持者认为 ________，但我怀疑是否 ________。

102. Obviously, ________ is good in many aspects. However, the other side of the coin voices its strong opposition.

很明显，________ 在很多方面具有优点，但其反对者的呼声也很强烈。

103. On the surface of it, this may seem to be a sound solution, but if thinking again, we would point out some drawbacks.

表面上看，这是一个合理的解决方案，但再一想，我们还是能指出一些缺点。

104. On the surface of it, this suggestion seems to be attractive, but thinking again, we would find it may lead to a set of problems.

表面上看，这个建议很吸引人，但是反复考虑，我们发现它可能带来很多问题。

105. Personally, I am in favour of the former point of view.

我个人更喜欢第一个观点。

106. Personally, I am standing on the side of ________.

我个人站在 ________ 一边。

107. Personally, I hold that ________.

我个人认为 ________。

108. Personally, I prefer ________. I think ________ has more advantages.

我个人更倾向于 ________，我认为 ________ 有更多的优点。

109. Personally, I side with the latter opinion.

我个人更倾向于后一种意见。

110. Personally, I stand on the side of the latter.

我个人支持后一种观点。

111. Personally, I would prefer ________ because I think ________ has more advantages.

我个人更喜欢 ________，因为我认为 ________ 有更多的优点。

112. Some people argue as if it is a general truth that ________. But to be frank, I cannot agree with them for the following reasons.

一些人议论 ________，好像这是一个普遍的事实。但坦率地说，以下原因使我不能同意这种说法。

113. Some people think ________. My opinion is identical with theirs.

一些人认为 ________。我的观点和他们的观点完全一致。

114. Sound and attractive as their arguments may seem, they cannot bear closer analysis.

尽管他们的论点是如此的合理和吸引人，但这些观点却经不起进一步的分析。

115. Superficially, all the above sounds reasonable and constructive. However, I strongly disagree with it.

表面上看，以上观点很合理，很有建设性。但是，我强烈反对。

116. Superficially, it seems to be a solution, but when carefully weighing in mind, we find that ________.

表面上看，它似乎是一个解决方案，但仔细考虑后，我们发现 ________。

117. Superficially, the above sounds reasonable and interesting. But when carefully weighing in mind, we find that it goes against the fact.

表面上看，上述观点很合理，也很吸引人，但经过仔细考虑后，我们发现它违背事实。

118. Taking into consideration both sides of the issue, I tend to favour the latter view.

考虑到双方的观点，我倾向于后者。

119. The advantages claimed for ________ over ________ are now being debated. Nonetheless, measure for measure, I confess that ________ is more advantageous.

________ 比 ________ 优点更多的结论现在是有争议的。但是，衡量再衡量，我承认，________ 有更多的优势。

120. The advantages of ________ always outweigh its disadvantages.

________ 总是利大于弊。

121. The advantages of ________ carry more weight than those of ________.

________ 的优点比 ________ 的多。

122. The other side of the coin has voiced strong opinion saying that ________.

反对方强烈地表示了反对意见，认为 ________。

123. There is no evidence to suggest that ________.

没有证据表明 ________。

124. There is some truth in these arguments, but they overlook a deeper and more basic factor that ________.

这些争论有其正确之处，但它们却忽略了更深一层的和更基本的因素：________。

125. Thinking logically, I can only say that the statement is valid.

从逻辑上考虑，我只能说这个观点是有根据的。

126. Though ________ has some advantages and it is popular to some extent, ________ will continue to play a more important role and will not fade out in people's life.

虽然 ________ 有一些优点，并且在一定程度上很受欢迎，但 ________ 将继续起到更重要的作用，而不会从人们的生活中消失。

127. Though the opinion stated above seems to have some merits, it overlooks some deeper and more basic factors.

虽然以上的意见有一些可取之处，但它没有注意到更深层次的和更基本的因素。

128. To be frank, I cannot agree with their opinion for the reasons below.

坦率地说，我不能同意这个意见，原因如下。

129. To choose ________ or ________ is a dilemma to the public, because they sometimes are confused by the seemingly good qualities of ________, and neglect the genuinely good aspects of ________.

公众在 ________ 和 ________ 的选择上感到棘手，因为他们有时候被 ________ 表面上的优点所蒙蔽，而忽视了 ________ 的真实优点。

130. To be frank, the advantages far outweigh the drawbacks.

坦率地说，优点远远多于缺点。

131. To suggest that ________ is the most obvious kind of nonsense.

________ 的建议显而易见是胡说。

132. Until recently, ________ was viewed as the prime argument. But people are taking a fresh

look at it.

直到最近，________ 还被看作是主要的理由；不过，人们对此有了全新的认识。

133. When considering opinions of both sides, I am inclined to take sides with the latter.

考虑过双方的观点后，我倾向于后一种观点。

134. When faced with ________, we find comfort in the idea that ________.

当面对 ________，我们拥护 ________ 的观点。

135. When faced with the decision of ________ or ________, quite a few would claim that ________, but others, in contrast, deem ________ as the premier choice and that is also my point.

当要在 ________ 和 ________ 中作出选择时，不少人认为 ________，但另一些人却相反，把 ________ 作为首选，这也是我的观点。

136. When it comes to ________, the majority would support ________. Others, however, like me, regard ________ as the propensity.

当谈到 ________ 时，大多数人支持 ________。但是另一些人，比如我，更倾向于 ________。

137. When it comes to ________, we find comfort in the idea that ________.

当谈到 ________ 时，我们更中意 ________。

138. While ________ has many merits to our lives, its drawbacks should not be ignored.

________ 对我们的生活有诸多好处，但是它的缺点也不容忽视。

139. While it is indispensable to mankind, it also brings us serious problems.

虽然它对人类而言是不可缺少的，但它也给我们带来很严重的问题。

140. While the majority may stick to the idea of ________, I would like to prefer ________.

当大多数人坚持 ________ 的观点时，我更倾向于 ________。

141. With views of both sides considered, I think that ________.

两方面都考虑之后，我认为 ________。

142. Yet I am one of many people who feel that ________.

而我是支持 ________ 的人之一。

143. Yet I am, and probably will always be, a deep lover of ________.

然而，我是，也可能永远是 ________ 的深爱者。

（三）开头段和理由段之间的过渡句

1. A number of reasons account for my point.

有很多的理由能说明我的观点。

2. Among countless factors which influence my decision, there are two or three conspicuous aspects.
在无数个影响我的决定的因素中，有两三个显而易见的因素。
3. And I would like to present two explanations to prove that I am right.
我愿意说出两个原因来证明我是对的。
4. But the problems I have with the above statement are as follows.
但我对上述观点的质疑如下。
5. I believe that I have found some solid advantages.
我相信我已经找到了一些可靠的优点。
6. I can see that many of the advantages of ________ seem obvious.
我能看到 ________ 有许多似乎显而易见的优点。
7. I support this with the following reasons.
我支持它的原因如下。
8. My arguments for this point are listed as follows.
关于这个观点，我的论述如下。
9. The following reasons should be taken into consideration.
必须考虑下列因素。
10. The reasons are chiefly as follows.
原因主要有以下几方面。
11. The reasons are presented below.
原因如下。
12. There are many instances in our daily life that can verify this.
在我们的日常生活中，有很多实例能够证明这一点。
13. There are many instances supporting my view.
有很多实例支持我的观点。
14. There are no less than three advantages in ________ as rendered below.
________ 的优点不少于三个，如下所述。
15. There are numerous reasons why I advocate the argument of ________, and I would explore a few of the most important ones here.
我赞同 ________ 的观点有很多原因，我将说明其中最重要的几个。
16. There are three advantages of ________ as follows.
________ 有三个好处，如下所示。
17. There are three premier causes as follows.
三个主要原因如下。

18. This quite different view is based on the following points.
这一截然不同的看法基于以下几点原因。
19. This view is based on the propensity of following points.
这个看法基于以下几点倾向。
20. To assume that ________ is destined to miss the following points.
假设 ________ 注定会忽略以下几点。

（四）理由段的主题句

1. A further reason why I prefer ________ is that ________.
我倾向 ________ 的一个更进一步的原因是 ________。
2. A more essential factor why I advocate the argument is that ________.
我同意这个观点的一个更根本的原因是 ________。
3. A more personal reason why I like ________ is that ________.
我喜欢 ________ 的另一个个人的原因是 ________。
4. A particularly notable case of this matter is ________.
这件事特别值得注意的地方是 ________。
5. ________ also deserves to mention here.
________ 也值得在这里提到。
6. Also, it is arbitrary to judge ________ according only to the excuse I mentioned in the above paragraph.
仅凭我上面阐述的理由就判断 ________ 是武断的。
7. Another benefit of ________, which ________ almost cannot achieve, is that ________.
________ 的另一个好处，也是 ________ 几乎不能达到的，是 ________。
8. Another factor shows that ________.
另一个因素说明 ________。
9. Another factor that should be taken into consideration is ________.
另一个需要考虑的因素是 ________。
10. Another innate characteristic of ________ is ________.
________ 的另一个本质特征是 ________。
11. Another reason why I advocate the attitude of ________ is that ________.
我赞成 ________ 态度的另一个原因是 ________。
12. Another reason why I agree with the above statement is that I believe ________.

我同意上述观点的另一个原因是我相信 ________。

13. Another reason why I dispute the above statement is that I believe that ________.
我怀疑上述观点的另一个原因是，我认为 ________。

14. Another reason why I prefer the argument is that ________.
我赞同这个观点的另一个原因是 ________。

15. Another reason why I would usually prefer to ________ is that ________.
我通常倾向于 ________ 的另一个原因是 ________。

16. As an individual, I feel that ________.
站在个人立场上，我认为 ________。

17. At the risk of sounding too simplistic, it seems to me that the main propositions can be summarised in one sentence.
也许听起来过于简单化，对我来说，主要原因可以被归结为一句话。

18. Beyond enormous obvious reasons, there lies a more in-depth cause.
除了许多显而易见的原因外，还有一个更深层次的原因。

19. But there is a more subtle point we must consider.
但是有一个更微妙的观点我们必须考虑到。

20. Certainly no other reason in my decision is more crucial than the one as follows.
我的决定中没有其他原因比这一个更关键。

21. Finally, the incomparable advantage of ________ is that ________.
最后，________ 的不可比拟的好处是 ________。

22. First, we can observe easily that ________.
首先，我们能容易地观察到 ________。

23. From a ________ （e.g. personal or psychological）perspective, I also prefer to ________ because ________.
从一个 ________（例如：个人的或心理上的）角度，我也倾向于 ________，因为 ________。

24. ________ has the benefit/advantage that ________.
________ 所具备的优点是 ________。

25. ________ has also had a bad effect on ________.
________ 对 ________ 还有一个不良的影响。

26. I agree with the above statement because I believe that ________.
我同意上面的论述，因为我认为 ________。

27. I agree with the statement without reservation since ________.

我毫无保留地同意这个观点，因为 ________。

28. I can see that one of the advantages of ________ seems obvious.

我能看到 ________ 的一个优势是显而易见的。

29. I disagree with the view because I consider ________.

我不同意这个观点，因为我认为 ________。

30. I have found a solid advantage.

我发现了一个实在的好处。

31. If we turn our attention to ________, we see that ________.

如果把我们的注意力转移到 ________ 上，我们可以看到 ________。

32. In terms of reality, the reason mentioned below seems advisable and deserves more consideration.

实际上，下面提及的原因有道理，值得仔细考虑。

33. ________ is superior in another way, that is ________.

________ 在另一个方面占优势，那就是 ________。

34. ________ is preferable to ________ because ________.

________ 比 ________ 更好，因为 ________。

35. It even might be said that ________.

甚至可以说 ________。

36. It is an obvious fact that ________.

________ 是一个显然的事实。

37. It is very clear that ________.

________ 是很清楚的。

38. It might also be noted that ________.

也可以注意到 ________。

39. Last but not the least, ________.

最后但并非最不重要的一点是，________。

40. Likewise, common sense tells us that ________.

同样，常识告诉我们 ________。

41. Moving on to wider themes, ________.

让我们转移到更广泛的主题，________。

42. No one could neglect/deny the fact that ________.

没人能忽视／否认 ________ 这一事实。

43. One of the most attractive points is that ________.

最吸引人的一个观点是 ________。

44. One of the most important things about ________ is that ________.

关于 ________ 的最重要的一点是 ________。

45. One of the notorious disadvantages of ________ is that ________.

________ 的一个众所周知的缺点是 ________。

46. One of the primary causes is that ________.

一个主要原因是 ________。

47. One of the reasons that are given for ________ is that ________.

________ 的一个原因是 ________。

48. One of the strengths of ________ is that ________.

________ 的一个优点是 ________。

49. One very strong argument for ________ is that ________.

________ 的一个非常有力的证据是 ________。

50. Perhaps another reason why ________ is superior to ________ lies in the fact that ________.

也许 ________ 优于 ________ 的另一个原因在于 ________。

51. Perhaps the most telling is ________.

也许最说明问题的是 ________。

52. Perhaps this is because of the simple fact that ________.

也许这是因为这一简单的事实：________。

53. Similarly, these reasons are also usable when we consider that ________.

同样地，当我们考虑 ________ 时，这些原因同样可用。

54. The above point is certainly true if ________ is considered.

如果考虑到 ________，上述观点一定正确。

55. The argument I support in the first paragraph is also in an advantageous position because ________.

在第一段中我支持的观点同样占优势，因为 ________。

56. The first and most important reason is that ________.

第一个也是最重要的原因是 ________。

57. The first reason can be seen by everyone.

第一个原因每个人都能看到。

58. The last factor to be taken seriously is ________.

最后一个需要认真考虑的因素是 ________。

59. The main problem with this argument is that it is ignorant of the basic fact that ________.
这个论点的主要问题是它忽视了 ________ 这一基本事实。

60. The main reason for my propensity is that ________.
我这种倾向的主要原因是 ________。

61. The main reason why I prefer ________ is that ________.
我倾向 ________ 的主要原因是 ________。

62. The most important benefit of ________ is that ________.
________ 的最重要的好处是 ________。

63. The problem I have with the above statement is that ________.
我对上述观点的质疑是 ________。

64. The reason why I disagree ________ is that ________.
我不同意 ________ 的原因是 ________。

65. The reasons are quite clear. Above all, ________.
原因非常清楚。首先，________。

66. The reasons for ________ are varied, nevertheless, they lie in the fact that ________.
________ 的原因是各式各样的，不过，它们基于这一事实：________。

67. The second reason for my propensity for ________ is that ________.
我倾向于 ________ 的第二个原因是 ________。

68. The second thing that must be taken into consideration is that ________.
必须考虑的第二个因素是 ________。

69. The third and very important reason is that ________.
第三个非常重要的原因是 ________。

70. The third, not the last, is that ________.
第三点，但不是最后一点，是 ________。

71. The undeniable deficiency in this remark is that it is negligent of the bare fact that ________.
这个论述中不可否认的缺陷就是它忽视了 ________ 这一显而易见的事实。

72. There is another factor that deserves some words here.
另一个原因值得在此说一说。

73. There is another obvious advantage for ________, that is ________.
________ 还有另一个明显的优势，那就是 ________。

74. Those who object to this idea forget a universal truth.
反对这个观点的人忘却了一个普遍真理。

75. To make a moral sense, I think that another reason why I prefer the argument of ________ is

that ________.

从道义上来说，我认为我倾向 ________ 观点的另一个原因是 ________。

76. We may look into every possible reason, however, the foremost reason for ________ is ________.

我们可以审视每一个可能的原因，但是，________ 的首要原因是 ________。

77. We should not lose sight of the fact that ________.

我们不能忽视这样的事实：________。

78. What is also worth noticing is that ________.

另一个值得注意的事情是 ________。

79. What is interesting is that ________.

有趣的是，________。

（五）举例

1. An example can give the details of this argument, ________.

一个例子能说明这个论点的详情，________。

2. An example of this fact is ________.

这个论据的一个事例是 ________。

3. An example to show this can be found in the story that ________.

说明这个问题的一个例子可以从 ________ 的故事中找到。

4. An instance that accompanies this reason is that ________.

一个可以说明这个原因的例子是 ________。

5. As I remember, ________.

根据我的记忆，________。

6. For example, ________.

例如，________。

7. For instance, ________.

例如，________。

8. History presented many examples of ________.

历史提供了许多 ________ 方面的事例。

9. I can give you another illustration about it, ________.

我可以给你提供另一个关于它的事例，________。

10. I can quote a common example, ________.

引用一个常见事例，________。

11. I have a bad experience with it.
关于它我有一段不愉快的经历。

12. In fact, a good example of this is that ________.
事实上，关于这点一个很好的事例是 ________。

13. In order to see this point clearly, let us see an example: ________.
为把这点看得更清楚，让我们看一个事例：________。

14. ________ is an outstanding example.
________ 是一个显著的例子。

15. It can be given a concrete example.
可以举一个具体事例。

16. It is a forceful example to demonstrate the importance of ________.
一个有力的例子能说明 ________ 的重要性。

17. It is best illustrated if given the following example.
下列的事例最能说明问题。

18. Let me give you an example, ________.
让我举个例子，________。

19. Let me provide an example.
让我给出一个事例。

20. Let's see an example.
让我们看一个例子。

21. Perhaps the most important example of ________ is that ________.
也许 ________ 最重要的例子是 ________。

22. Take ________ for an example, it is a very obvious case.
以 ________ 为例，这是一个显而易见的例子。

23. The modern example of this is ________.
关于这点，一个发生在现代的事例是 ________。

24. There is one impressive example I want to mention here.
我想给大家举一个印象深刻的例子。

25. To give some concrete examples, ________.
举一些具体事例，________。

26. To illustrate this, there is an example that is very persuasive.
为说明这一点，有一个例子非常具有说服力。

27. We could take ________ as an example, ________.
我们可以把 ________ 作为一个例子，________。

（六）结尾段

1. Admittedly, both sides are reasonable. But they are one-sided. In my opinion, ________.
不可否认，双方都有道理，但都很片面。我的意见是，________。
2. Admittedly, there are merits to both arguments. As far as I am concerned, I would like to take a more balanced position. That is to say, ________.
不可否认，两种论点都有自己的道理。就我而言，我将站在一个更中立的角度上，也就是说，________。
3. After understanding the reasoning above, it's quite safe now to say: to choose ________ is a wise action.
在了解上面的推理后，现在可以很肯定地说：选择 ________ 是明智的。
4. All in all/In summary/In sum/In conclusion/In short/In a word, ________.
总而言之/综上所述，________。
5. All in all, I should say that ________.
总之，我必须说 ________。
6. All in all, the advantages of ________ outweigh its disadvantages.
总之，________ 的优点多于它的缺点。
7. All reliable evidences point to one saying, that is ________.
所有可靠的证据证明了一句话，那就是 ________。
8. All the above opinions make sense. Therefore, it is really hard for me to draw a definite conclusion. Here I would like to take a more balanced position that ________.
上面所有的观点都有道理。因此我很难得出一个明确的结论。我愿意站在一个更中立的立场上，那就是 ________。
9. All the above suggests that we can come to the simple conclusion that ________.
以上所说的一切表明我们可以得出这样一个简单的结论，那就是 ________。
10. All the evidence justifies an unshakable view that ________.
所有的证据证明了一个不可动摇的观点，也就是 ________。
11. All the evidence supports an unmistakable conclusion that ________.
所有的证据证明了一个千真万确的结论，也就是 ________。
12. All the opinions above make sense, and consequently it is hard to come to an absolute

conclusion. In my opinion, ________.

上面所有的观点都有道理，因此很难得出绝对的结论。我的意见是，________。

13. All these opinions make sense, and consequently it is hard to decide which one is more reasonable.

所有这些意见都有道理，因此很难决定哪个更有道理。

14. As far as I am concerned, I think there is truth in the argument of these two parties. I would like to have a balanced view.

对我而言，我认为两方面的论述都有其正确性。我愿持一个平衡的看法。

15. Based on the above discussion and analysis, we can see that ________.

基于上述讨论和分析，我们可以看到 ________。

16. But all in all, I would say the advantages outweigh the disadvantages. With the advance of society, if we make full use of the merits and eliminate the drawbacks, all people will enjoy a better life.

但总而言之，利大于弊。随着社会进步，如果我们发扬优点，克服缺点，所有人都会过上更好的生活。

17. But if all these factors are contemplated carefully, the advantages of ________ carry more weight than those of ________.

但是，如果仔细考虑所有这些因素，________ 的好处超过 ________ 的好处。

18. Consequently, I strongly commit to the notion that ________.

因此，我强烈主张 ________。

19. For the reasons presented above, I strongly commit to the notion that ________.

根据上述理由，我坚决同意 ________ 的观点。

20. From the above comparison and contrast, anyone can safely conclude that ________.

通过以上的分析比较，任何人都可以肯定地认为 ________。

21. From what has been discussed above, I think the correct attitude is that ________.

通过上面的讨论，我想正确的态度是 ________。

22. From what has been discussed above, we can see ________ does more harm than good to us. Therefore, I strongly approve of the notion that ________.

从上面我们所讨论的内容可以看出 ________ 的弊大于利。因此，我坚决赞成 ________。

23. From what has been discussed above, we may finally draw the conclusion that ________.

根据上面所讨论的情况，我们最后可能得出这样的结论：________。

24. From what has been discussed above, we may safely arrive at the conclusion that ________.

从上面的讨论中，我们很自然地得出 ________ 这一结论。

25. From what has been mentioned above, we can clearly see that ________.

从上面我们所谈到的，我们能很清楚地看出 ________。

26. From what has been mentioned above, we may see that there is some truth in both arguments. Personally, I side with the latter opinion.

从以上的论述中，我们可以看到双方的论述都有些道理。我个人更支持后一种观点。

27. From what has been stated above, I suppose that ________.

基于上面的陈述，我认为 ________。

28. Given the factors I have just outlined, I can only say that ________.

有了我列举的多种因素，我只能说 ________。

29. I firmly commit to the notion that ________.

我的观点很鲜明，那就是 ________。

30. If considered seriously, ________.

如果认真考虑，________。

31. In a word, I can hardly share the proposal that ________.

一句话，我不能同意 ________ 的提议。

32. In conclusion, although ________ has its negative effects, it can, to a great extent, bring us more advantages.

总之，虽然 ________ 有其负面影响，但从很大程度上来说，它能给我们带来更多的好处。

33. In general/On the whole/Generally, ________.

总的说来，________。

34. It is not difficult to get the conclusion that ________.

不难得出 ________ 这一结论。

35. It is obvious for us to conclude that ________.

对我们来说，显然可以得出 ________ 的结论。

36. It is safe to draw the conclusion that ________.

很自然地得出 ________ 的结论。

37. It is sagacious to support the statement that ________.

支持 ________ 的观点是明智的。

38. Judging from all evidence offered, we may reasonably come to/draw the conclusion that ________.

从所提供的证据来看，我们可以得出这样的结论，也就是 ________。

39. Now, after close examination, it is not difficult to draw the conclusion that only choosing ________ is sensible.

现在，在仔细考虑后，不难得出这个结论：只选择 ________ 是明智的。

40. Once you have known all of these, you must agree with me that ________ is right.
如果你知道所有这些，你一定和我一样会同意 ________ 是对的。

41. Recognising the fact that ________ should drive us to conclude that ________.
意识到 ________ 这样的事实，可以让我们得出 ________ 的结论。

42. So from what has been discussed, one can only reach this conclusion: ________.
所以，根据上面所讨论的情况，人们只能得出这一结论：________。

43. So if we take a careful consideration, it is not difficult to get the conclusion: ________.
所以，如果我们认真考虑一下，不难得出这样的结论：________。

44. So, as I see it, ________.
所以，正像我所看到的，________。

45. So, based on the above discussion, I agree with the opinion that ________.
所以，基于上述讨论，我同意 ________ 这一意见。

46. So, in comparison with ________, ________ is surely a clever choice.
所以，和 ________ 相比，________ 确实是一个聪明的选择。

47. Taking account of all these factors, we may reach the conclusion that ________.
考虑到所有这些因素，我们能得出这样的结论，也就是 ________。

48. Taking all these factors into consideration, we may reasonably come to the conclusion that ________.
考虑到所有的这些因素，我们可以合理地得出 ________ 的结论。

49. Taking into account the arguments of both sides, I think ________.
考虑到双方的论点，我认为 ________。

50. There is no question in my mind that ________.
________ 在我看来是没有问题的。

51. There is probably a little bit of truth in both arguments and the opinions stated by both sides make sense and consequently, it is hard to choose the better one of them.
两方面的论点和观点都有些道理，因此，很难从中选出更好的一个。

52. There is probably a little bit of truth in both arguments. For my part, I completely agree with the latter.
两种观点都有道理。站在我的立场上，我完全同意后者。

53. Therefore, it is not difficult for us to come to the conclusion that ________.
因此，我们不难得出 ________ 的结论。

54. To put all into a nutshell, I ________.

简而言之，我 ________。

55. To sum up, I feel that, overall, there are strong positive effects of ________.

总之，我认为 ________ 总体上有很大的积极作用。

56. To sum up, we cannot deny that both sides are well-grounded. In my opinion, ________.

总之，双方的论据都很充分。我的观点是 ________。

57. We may discover that ________.

我们可以发现 ________。

58. What we must do is to encourage the strengths and diminish the weaknesses to the least extent.

我们必须做的是发挥长处，最大限度地克服不足。

59. When the advantages and disadvantages are carefully compared, the most striking conclusion is self-evident.

在仔细地比较了优缺点之后，最有力的结论就不言而喻了。

60. With the views of both sides considered, I think that ________.

考虑双方的观点后，我认为 ________。

第四章　图表写作

一、概述

雅思写作考试学术类的第一篇是写一篇图表作文，即要求对图表进行描述、解释和说明。

（一）字数和时间要求

字数要求在 150 词以上，一般不要超过 200 词。
学术类写作的两篇文章的时间一共是 60 分钟。建议考生的图表写作用时 20–25 分钟左右。

（二）图表类型

雅思写作考试的图表写作部分所提供的图表一般分为以下两种：
1. 统计数据图表，占 80% 以上；
2. 过程图及地图，占不到 20%。

（三）写作格式

和议论文一样，图表作文分为缩进式和齐头式两种。

下面，分别介绍统计数据图表、过程图和地图的写法。

二、统计数据图表

（一）分类

统计数据图表可分为如下四种：
1. table（表格）
2. line graph（曲线图）
3. bar chart/column graph（直方图/柱状图）
4. pie chart（饼图）

（二）结构

图表作文一般可写2-4段。

1. 第一段：引言0-2句

如果图表信息多，主体段落有充足的内容可写，开头段也可以不写。如果写的话，一般是用1-2句话，改写题目中的文字说明。

2. 主体段落：根据具体情况，写1-3段。

（1）两个图表的

通常是一个图表一段，如果两个图表的关系比较密切（这样的图表不太多），可再写一段比较两个图表中的数据。

（2）一个图表的

分两种情况：

第一种情况：图表中有不同的时间，先用一到两段分别描述各个对象在不同时间的变化，再用一段对各对象进行比较。

第二种情况：图表中没有不同的时间，按描述对象分段，如果描述对象多于三个，把相似的对象合为一段来写。

（3）三或四个图表的

这种情况很少，没有什么共同规律，根据具体情况分为1-3段。

3. 结尾段 0-2句

指出图表所要说明的道理，但很多图表不用写结尾段。

下面，结合考试真题进行讲解，前面的范文给出了分析说明。

Topic 1 生活质量统计表

You should spend about 20 minutes on this task.

The following table gives statistics showing the aspects of quality of life in five countries.

Summarise the information by selecting and reporting the main features, and make comparisons where relevant.

Write at least 150 words.

Selected statistics showing aspects of the quality of life in five countries

Country	GNP per head (1982: US dollars)	Daily calorie supply per head	Life expectancy at birth (years)	Infant mortality rate (per 1,000 live births)
Bangladesh	140	1,877	40	132
Bolivia	570	2,086	50	124
Egypt	690	2,950	56	97
Indonesia	580	2,296	49	87
USA	13,160	3,652	74	12

Sample Answer

The USA had the highest GNP per head and daily calorie intake, the longest life expectancy and the lowest infant mortality rate. In 1982, its GNP per head was 13,160 US dollars, but its infant mortality rate was only 12 per 1,000 live births.

Egypt, Indonesia and Bolivia were similar in those four indicators. As a whole, Egypt had the highest quality of life among the three countries. It had the highest figure in three indicators: GNP per head, daily calorie supply per head and life expectancy at birth. In 1982, its GNP per head was 690 US dollars, whereas those of Indonesia and Bolivia were 580 and 570 US dollars respectively. However, Indonesia's infant mortality rate was 87 per 1,000, which was slightly lower than that of Egypt (97) and that of Bolivia (124).

Bangladesh had the lowest quality of life in the five countries. Its GNP per head was nearly 100 times smaller than that of USA. The figures in terms of the daily calorie supply per head and life expectancy at birth in Bangladesh were only the half of those respectively in the USA. And its infant mortality rate was 11 times greater.

分析说明：

1. 结构

这一图表没有不同的时间，所以按描述对象分段。一共有五个对象（五个国家），但不能写五段。通过分析图表，可以发现美国一枝独秀，中间三个国家相似，第一个国家，虽然很可能不认识这个词（孟加拉国），但它的情况最差。所以可以写三段：美国一段，中间三个国家一段，孟加拉国一段。这篇范文没有写开头段和结尾段。

2. 常用句型

（1）The USA had the highest GNP per head and daily calorie intake, the longest life expectancy and the lowest infant mortality rate.

美国有最高的人均 GNP 和日常的热量摄入，最长的平均寿命和最低的婴儿死亡率。

句型分析：

通过这句话考生可以学习最高级的表达方法，同时要注意这句话使用的是一般过去时，因为图表通常描述的是过去的情况。所以通常情况下，描述数据要使用一般过去时。

（2）In 1982, its GNP per head was 13,160 US dollars, but its infant mortality rate was only 12 per 1,000 live births.

1982 年，美国的人均 GNP 是 13,160 美元，但是婴儿死亡率仅仅是 12‰。

句型分析：

通过这句话考生可以学习具体数据的表达方法，同时要注意转折词 but 的使用——在描述统计数据的图表时，经常使用表示转折关系的关联词。

（3）As a whole, Egypt had the highest quality of life among the three countries.

总体上，埃及是这三个国家之中生活质量最高的。

句型分析：

本句是描述最高级的句型。as a whole 的意思是“总体上说，大体上讲”。在描述统计数据的图表时，这个词组经常能用到。

（4）However, Indonesia's infant mortality rate was 87 per 1,000, which was slightly lower than that of Egypt (97) and that of Bolivia (124).

印度尼西亚的婴儿死亡率是 87‰，这比埃及（97‰）和玻利维亚（124‰）略低。

句型分析：

通过这句话，可以学习具体数据的描述，定语从句的使用，比较级的使用，以及用括号括注具体数据。slightly lower 的意思是“低一点点”，much lower 的意思是“低很多”。that 在这里指代 infant mortality rate，这种指代方法在描述统计数据的图表中使用较多。

（5）Its GNP per head was nearly 100 times smaller than that of the USA.

它的人均 GNP 几乎只是美国的 1%。

句型分析：

通过这句话考生可以学习倍数的描述方法，句子的结构通常为：数字 + times + 形容词（副词）比较级 + than...。

Topic 2 电视和收音机受众的统计曲线图

You should spend about 20 minutes on this task.

The graph below shows radio and television audiences throughout the day in 1992.

Summarise the information by selecting and reporting the main features, and make comparisons where relevant.

Write at least 150 words.

Radio and television audiences in the UK, October, December 1992

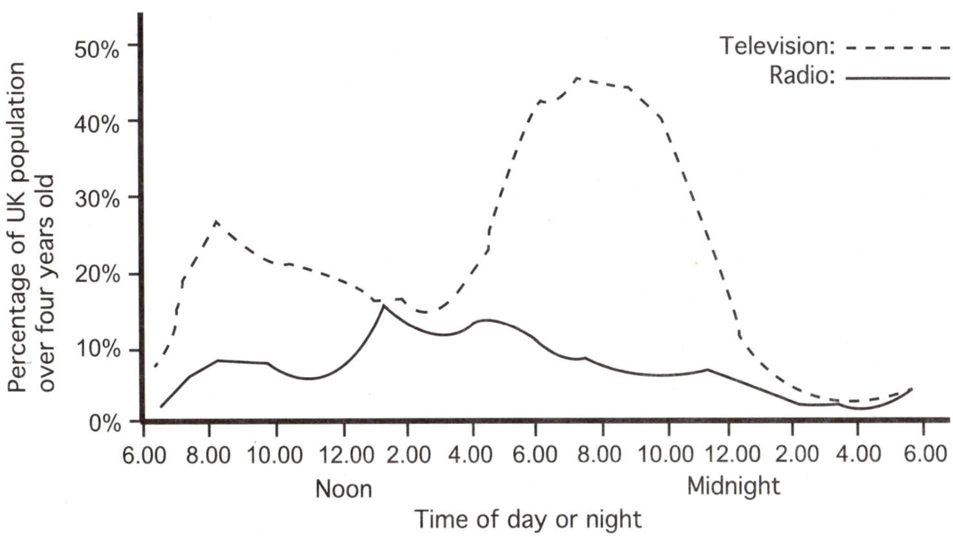

Sample Answer

The graph shows the percentage of the UK population over the age of four years old that listened to the radio and watched television throughout the day in 1992.

The number of TV audiences increased rapidly from 6:00 a.m. to 8:00 a.m. At 8:00 a.m., it reached its first highest point at nearly 30%. Then, for the rest of the day, the number dropped gradually, with a slight increase around 3:00 p.m. After that, the number of TV audiences rose sharply until 8:00 p.m., peaking nearly at 50%. From then, the number fell rapidly until around 4:00 a.m. next morning.

Unlike television, there was a slight increase in the number of radio audiences from about 3% at 6:00 a.m. to about 7% at 8:00 a.m. From 8:00 a.m. to about 10:00 a.m., it remained almost stable. From then on, the number dropped slightly at first and then rose steadily till about 1:00 p.m., peaking at 16%. Then it dropped gradually until 4:00 a.m. next morning.

Around 1:00 p.m., the number of people listening to the radio was nearly equal to that of people watching TV. However, for the rest of the day, much more UK audiences chose to watch TV rather than listen to the radio. As a whole, throughout the whole day, the average number of TV audiences was larger than that of the radio.

分析说明：

1. 结构

写了一个开头段，改写题目中的文字说明。这是一个标有不同时间段的图表。先用两段分别描述电视和收音机的人数在一天中的变化规律，然后再用一段对它们进行比较。

2. 常用句型

（1）At 8:00 a.m., it reached its first highest point at nearly 30%.
看电视的人数在早晨 8 点的时候达到第一次高峰，接近 30%。

句型分析：
通过这句话考生可以学习一种描述数据达到最高点的方法。the highest point 是"最高点"的意思。"最低点"的表述是 the lowest point。

（2）After that, the number of TV audiences rose sharply until 8:00 p.m., peaking nearly at 50%.
之后，看电视的人数急速增加，在晚上 8 点的时候达到一个高峰，接近 50%。

句型分析：
通过这句话考生可以学到一种描述数据上升、下降的方法，即：变化的对象 + 动词 + 副词。同样要注意时态。peaking nearly at 50% 在这里是分词短语作状语，peak 是"达到最高点"的意思。

（3）Unlike television, there was a slight increase in the number of radio audiences from about 3% at 6:00 a.m. to about 7% at 8:00 a.m.
与电视不同，从早上 6 点到 8 点收听收音机的人的比例只有小幅的增长，从 3% 增长到 7%。

句型分析：

通过这句话考生学习一种描述数据上升、下降的方法，即：there be + 形容词 + 名词 + in + 变化的对象。同样，请考生在描述时注意时态。

（4）From 8:00 a.m. to about 10:00 a.m., it remained almost stable.
从早上8点到10点左右则基本保持不变。

句型分析：

通过这句话考生可以学习如何描述数据保持不变，remain stable用得很好。

（5）Around 1:00 p.m., the number of people listening to the radio was nearly equal to that of people watching TV.
在下 午1点左右，收听收音机的人数几乎和看电视的人数持平。

句型分析：

通过这句话考生可以学习描述数据不差上下的方法。listening to the radio 和 watching TV 是分词短语作后置定语。that 指代 the number。

Topic 3 监狱在押人员对比图

You should spend about 20 minutes on this task.

The bar chart below shows the figures for imprisonment in five countries between 1930 and 1980.

Write a report for a university lecturer describing the information shown below.

Write at least 150 words.

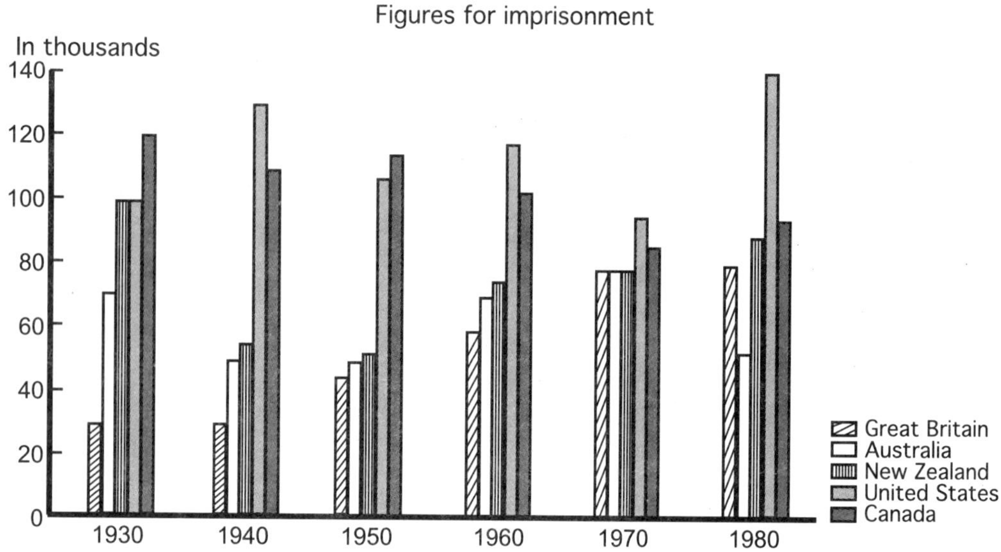

Sample Answer

The bar chart shows the figures for imprisonment in five countries from 1930 to 1980.

The number of prisoners in Great Britain increased from 30,000 in 1930 to 80,000 in 1980. The number of prisoners in Australia fell rapidly from 1930 to 1940, kept stable from 1940 to 1950, increased gradually till 1970 and then decreased sharply in 1980. The number of prisoners in New Zealand dropped sharply from 1930 to 1940, and remained stable till 1950, but then increased gradually to 1980.

The number of prisoners in the United States rose greatly from 1930 to 1940, and then decreased till 1950. After that, it increased slightly. The number decreased from 1960 to 1970, and then increased sharply by 1980. The number of prisoners in Canada decreased slightly from 1930 to 1940, and then increased slightly till 1950. The number decreased gradually from 1950 to 1970, and then increased a little from 1970 to 1980.

From 1930 to 1960, Great Britain had the lowest figure among the five countries. However, the number was increasing gradually year by year. In 1980, Australia had the lowest number. The country which had the highest number was either the United States or Canada. Canada had the highest number in 1930 and 1950. The United Sates had the highest number in the other years.

说明：

本文写了一个开头段，用来改写题目中的文字说明。这是一个标明了不同时间段的图表。先用两段分别描述五个国家入狱人数从 1930 年到 1980 年的变化规律。然后，再用一段对它们进行比较。

Topic 4 交通方式统计图

You should spend about 20 minutes on this task.

The bar chart shows the different modes of transport used to travel to and from work in one city in 1950, 1970 and 1990.

Write at least 150 words.

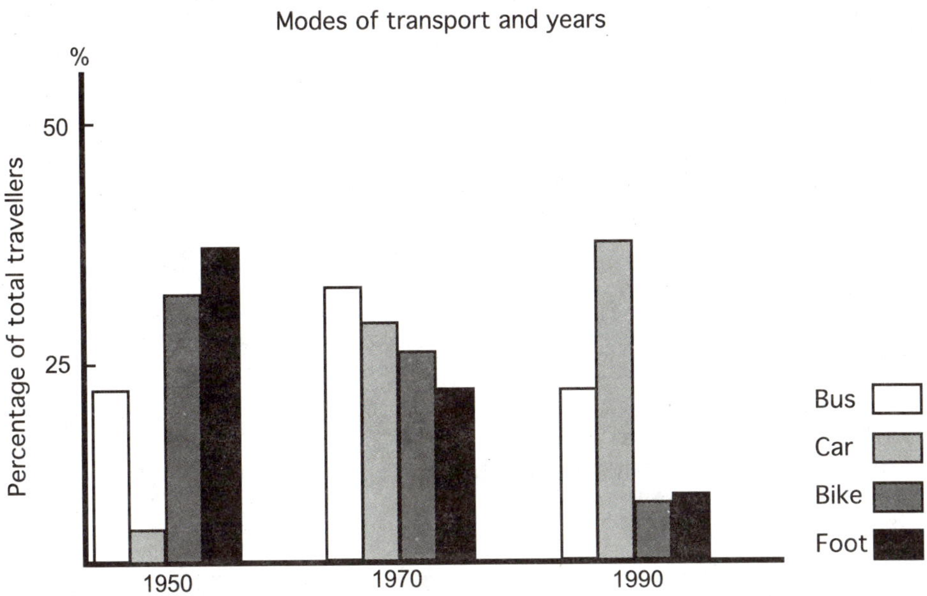

Sample Answer

According to the bar chart, there were many dramatic changes in the use of transport from 1950 to 1990.

The use of cars increased significantly from 1950 to 1990. In 1950, only a small amount of people drove to work. But, in 1970, more than one quarter of people owned a car. By 1990, the number of people who went to work by car jumped to almost 40%.

During the same period, there were gradual declines in the use of bicycle and foot. In 1950, more than 60% people were cycling or walking to work. In 1970, the use of bicycle or foot still occupied over 40%. But in 1990, the number of these people decreased to less than 25%.

The use of bus went up from 1950 to 1970 and went down to the original point from 1970 to 1990 (less than 25%).

The bar chart shows that automobiles had become the most popular vehicle by 1990.

Topic 5 男女职业分配比例图

You should spend about 20 minutes on this task.

The diagram below shows the distribution of men and women in key professions in Malaysia in 1970.

Describe the distribution of men and women in the professions in Malaysia, as indicated in the diagram.

Write at least 150 words.

Distribution of men and women in key professions in Malaysia in 1970

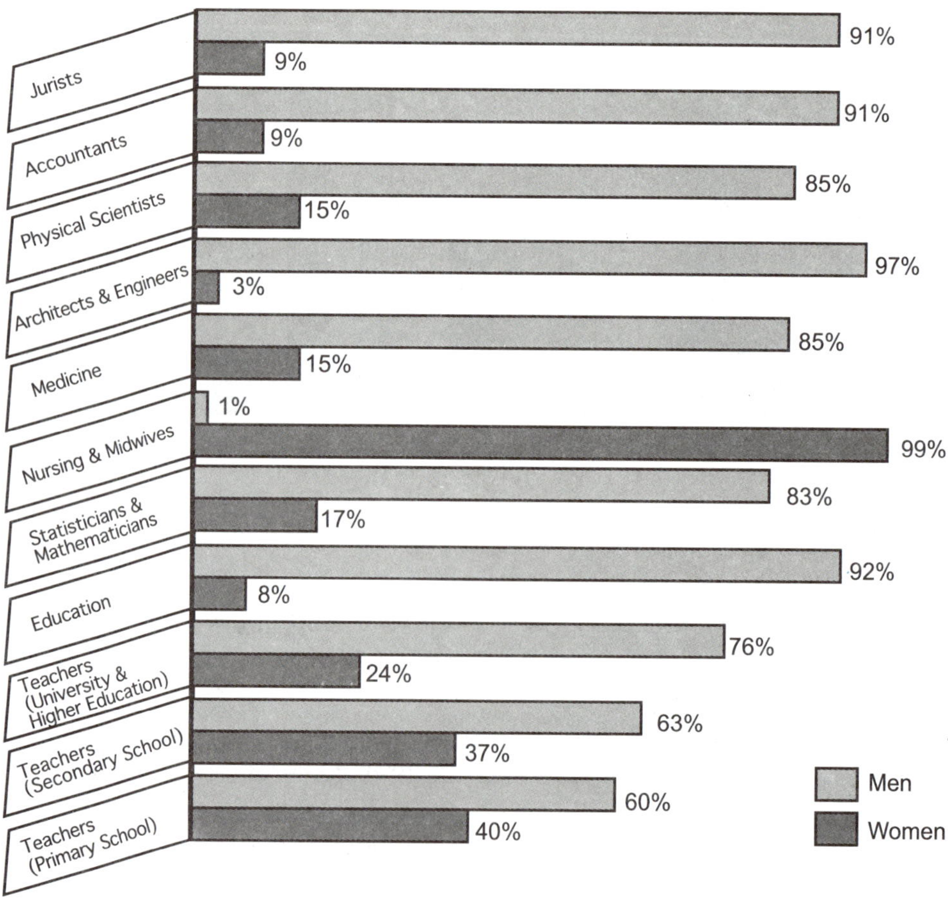

Sample Answer

The bar chart compares the male and female roles in key professions in Malaysia in 1970.

In 1970, most of the key professions in Malaysia were dominated by men. Men occupied more than 90% of the four key professions presented in this chart, including jurists, accountants, architects and engineers, and education. Architecture and engineering were particularly male-dominated, where men made up 97% while women only accounted for 3%.

Women were a little more active in physical science and medicine, comprising 15% respectively in these two fields. And 17% statisticians and mathematicians were women. Women had a comparatively high percentage rate in the field of teaching. However, an interesting fact is that the proportion decreased according to the level, from around 40% of teachers in primary schools to under 25% of teachers in universities and higher education. The only profession where women dominated was in nursing and midwives, the traditional female profession, with 99% of all nurses and midwives being women.

The diagram, therefore, shows that there existed serious sexual discrimination in employment in Malaysia in 1970.

Topic 6 英国居民出国旅行调查表

You should spend about 20 minutes on this task.

The first chart below shows the results of a survey which sampled a cross section of 100,000 people asked if they travelled abroad and why they travelled for the period 1994-1998. The second chart shows their destinations over the same period.

Write a report for a university lecturer describing the information shown below.

Write at least 150 words.

Visits abroad by UK residents by purpose of visit (1994–1998)

	1994	1995	1996	1997	1998
Holiday	15,246	14,898	17,896	19,703	20,700
Business	3,155	3,188	3,249	3,639	3,957
Visits to friends and relatives	2,689	2,628	2,774	3,051	1,181
Other reasons	982	896	1,030	1,054	990
Total	22,072	21,610	24,949	27,447	26,828

Destinations of visits abroad by UK residents in main regions (1994-1998)				
	Western Europe	North America	Other areas	Total
1994	19,371	919	1,782	22,072
1995	18,944	914	1,752	21,610
1996	21,877	1,167	1,905	24,949
1997	23,661	1,559	2,227	27,447
1998	24,519	1,823	2,486	28,828

Sample Answer

The first table reveals purposes for travel by UK residents from 1994 to 1998. The number of travellers for holiday decreased from 1994 to 1995, but then increased gradually, peaking at 20,700 in 1998. The number of travellers for business increased from 3,155 in 1994 to 3,957 in 1998. The number of people who went abroad to see friends and relatives remained stable from 1994 to 1997, while dropped sharply in 1998. The number of travellers for other purposes fluctuated around 1,000. Among the four purposes, holiday and business had the largest and second largest number respectively. Comparatively, a smaller number of people had been to other countries to see friends and relatives. Other purposes had the smallest number.

The second table indicates which areas UK residents visited during this period. The number of travellers to Western Europe increased from 19,371 in 1994 to 24,519 in 1998. The number of travellers to North America doubled from 919 in 1994 to 1,823 in 1998. The number of travellers to other areas increased from 1,782 in 1994 to 2,486 in 1998. Among the three destinations, Western Europe had the highest number and North America had the lowest number.

说明：

题目提供了两份图表，因为信息比较多，通常不需要写开头段。这两个图表没有密切的关系，所以一个图表写一段。每段先用一句话概述，然后再详细描述。

Topic 7　交流方式变化图

You should spend about 20 minutes on this task.

The two pie charts show the types of communication used in 1962 and in 1982.

Write a report to describe the information shown in the charts.

Write at least 150 words.

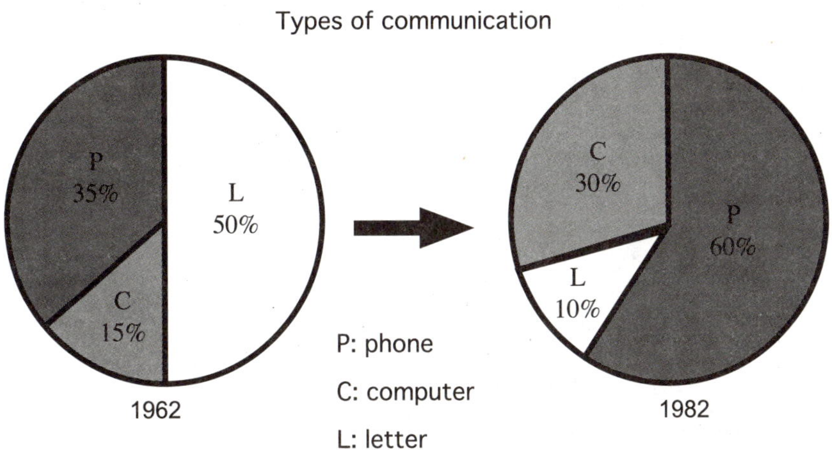

Sample Answer

The two pie charts compare different methods of communication used in 1962 and in 1982. We can see that there are significant changes for each medium surveyed.

In 1962, letter writing was the most popular form of communication, taking up 50% of the total. However, its use decreased dramatically after that. By 1982, this figure dropped to only 10%, the smallest of that year's figures for types of communication.

On the other hand, during this same period, we can see that the use of the phone and computer both increased significantly. In 1962, the use of telephone just occupied 35% and the computer was the least used form (15%) of the three methods. In 1982, the telephone, 60%, has become the most used form of communication. Similarly, the use of computers doubled to 30%.

Overall, we can see some important changes in the forms of communication used during the two decades. More and more people appreciate the convenience brought about by the phone and the computer.

Topic 8 癌症治疗效果图

You should spend about 20 minutes on this task.

The graphs below indicate the effect of treatment in two types of cancer in females.

Using the information in the graphs, describe and compare the situation with and without treatment for the two types of cancer.

Write at least 150 words.

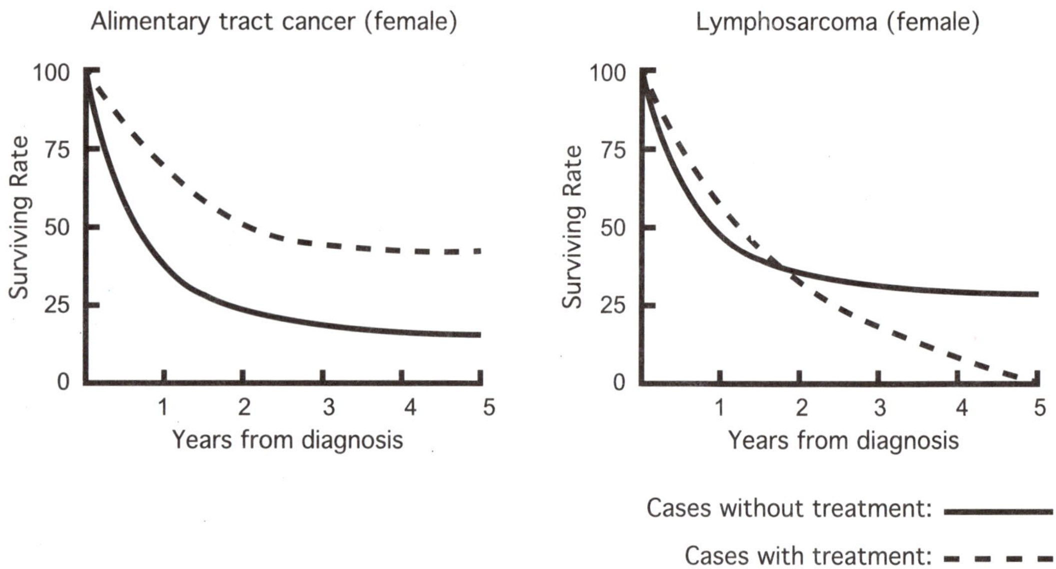

Sample Answer

The two graphs show the situation with and without treatment for two types of cancer in women: the alimentary tract cancer and lymphosarcoma.

For the alimentary tract cancer, treatment can be reasonably effective. Only 30% of patients survive the first year after diagnosis without treatment, while about 75% of patients survive when treatment is applied. Without treatment, less than 25% of patients survive for five years after diagnosis, but with treatment the survival rate after five years reaches nearly 50%.

For lymphosarcoma, however, treatment can have a negative effect. The survival rate one and a half years after diagnosis is around 40% whether treatment is applied or not. However, the survival rate with treatment is lower than that without treatment beyond one and a half years. After five years, more than 25% of untreated patients are still alive, whereas none of the patients who have received treatment survive for five years after diagnosis.

Topic 9 快餐消耗图

You should spend about 20 minutes on this task.

The chart below shows the amount of money per person per week spent on fast foods in Britain. The graph shows the trends in consumption of fast foods.

Write at least 150 words.

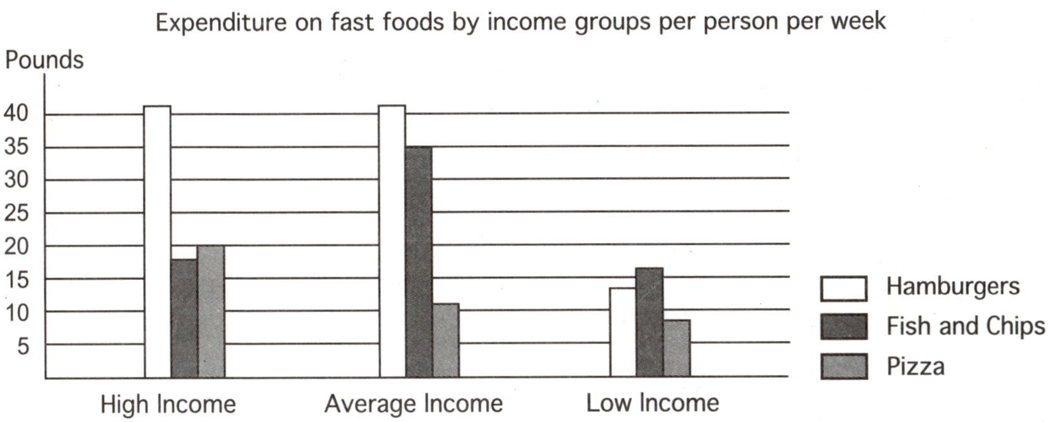

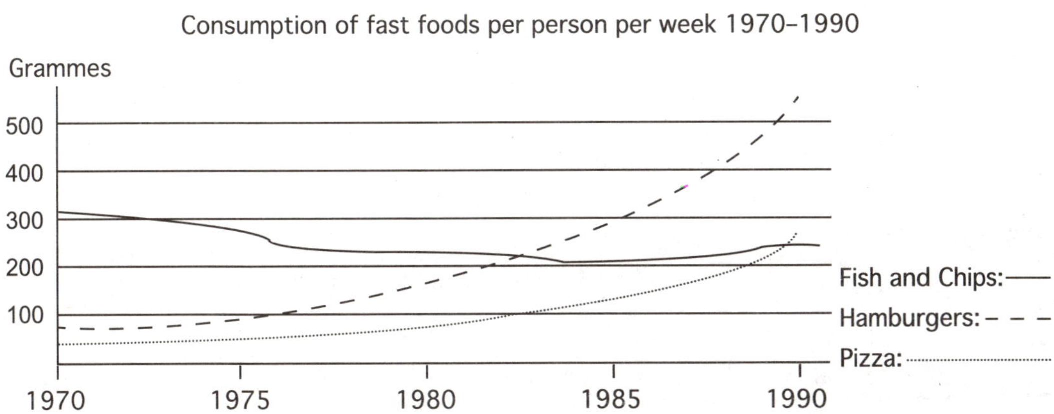

Sample Answer

The bar chart shows the amount of money expended on fast foods among three different income groups. Hamburgers are the most popular fast food in the high and average income groups. People in these two groups spend more than 40 pounds per person per week on the consumption of hamburgers. Although fish and chips is the most popular food for those in the low income group, it is the least popular for those in the high income group. Pizza, on the other hand, is not very popular among the average income group. It is obvious that people in the low income group spend much less money on fast foods.

The line graph indicates the general pattern of fast foods consumption between 1970 and 1990. Obviously, there was a sharp increase in the consumption of hamburgers during this period. In 1970, people in Britain ate less than 100 grammes of hamburgers per person per week. By 1990, this number increased to over 500 grammes. Pizza also increased but it was not so dramatic. Fish and chips, however, dropped slightly. Before around 1983, fish and chips was the most popular fast food. However, after that, hamburgers increased sharply and they became much more popular than the other two kinds of fast foods.

三、过程图及地图

在关于过程图及地图的写作过程中，要注意以下五点：

1. 看懂图表非常重要，通常需要花较多时间。
2. 主体段落通常只写一段，如果字数不够，可考虑写开头段和结尾段。
3. 有的图表需要先描述物体或机器的组成部分。
4. 选择逻辑上合理的开始点，顺着箭头方向，依次描述。
5. 充分利用图表中所给的词，图表中没有的词，尽量用一些简单的词汇，以保证正确性。

下面，来看几篇关于过程图及地图的写作范文。

Topic 10　冰箱工作原理图

You should spend about 20 minutes on this task.

Using the information in the diagram, write a description of how a refrigerator works.

You may use your own knowledge and experience in addition to the diagram.

Write at least 150 words.

How a refrigerator works

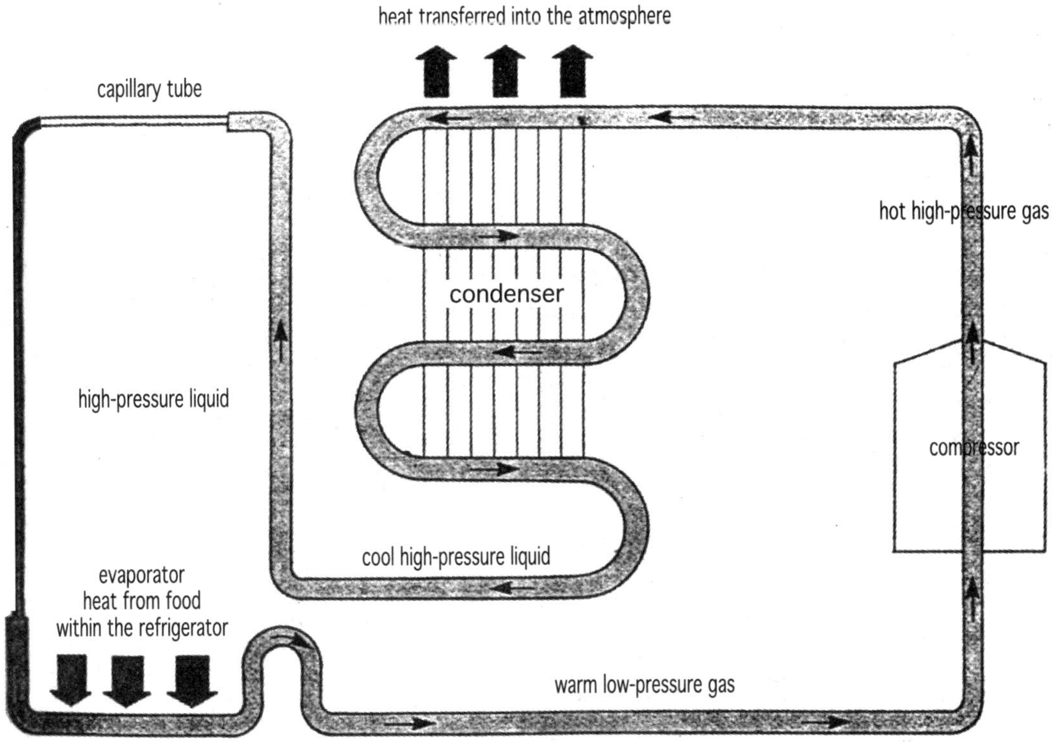

Sample Answer

The diagram shows the component parts of the refrigerating system of a refrigerator and how it works to keep a low temperature to store food.

A refrigerator has four main parts for refrigeration: a compressor, a condenser, a capillary tube and an evaporator. High-pressure liquid flows in the capillary tube first, then, it flows into the evaporator, where the high-pressure liquid is heated by heat from food within the refrigerator and turns into warm low-pressure gas. The warm low-pressure gas flows ahead and arrives at the compressor, where it is compressed to hot high-pressure gas. The next destination of the hot high-pressure gas is the condenser, in which it is turned into cool high-pressure liquid. Where is the heat then? It is transferred into the atmosphere. The cool high-pressure liquid continues to flow forward and enters into the capillary tube. It is heated in the evaporator by heat from food within the refrigerator again and a new cycle begins.

In this way, the food within the refrigerator is kept in a low temperature and, therefore, remains fresh.

说明：

写了开头段和结尾段。主体段落写一段，先写这个物体（冰箱）的组成部分，然后顺着箭头方向依次描述它的工作原理。

Topic 11　塑料制品循环图

You should spend about 20 minutes on this task.

As a class assignment you have been asked to write a description of how this plastic is produced and then broken down.

Using the information in the diagram, write a description of the cycle.

You may use your own knowledge and experience in addition to the diagram.

Write at least 150 words.

Plastic cycle

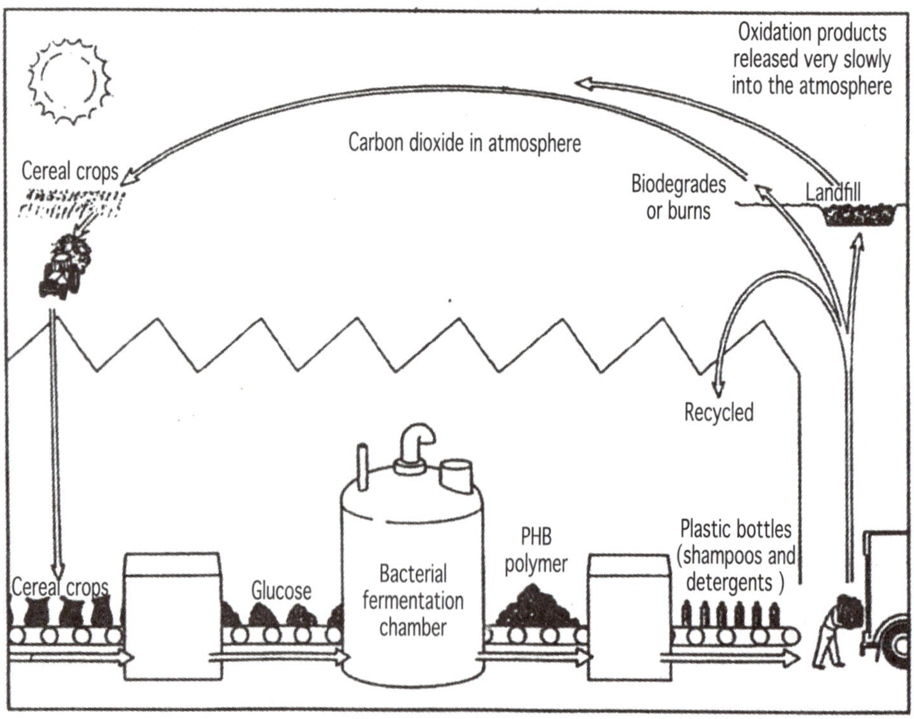

Sample Answer

Cereal crops are harvested from the fields and taken to a factory, where they are processed and glucose is extracted from them. The glucose then passes into a bacterial fermentation chamber, where the process of fermentation produces a type of plastic called PHB polymer. This can be used to make plastic bottles to hold shampoos and detergents. When these plastic bottles are thrown away, they may be recycled. In other words, they are used again in the same form. However, they may also be dumped in a landfill. In this case, they are digested by bacteria in the soil and broken down there. The oxidation products from the landfill sites are released slowly into the atmosphere. Other discarded bottles are burnt or biodegraded and send out carbon dioxide into the atmosphere. Cereal crops require carbon dioxide in order to grow, and these crops are used in the manufacture of the new plastic.

Topic 12 乡村发展图

You should spend about 20 minutes on this task.

Chorleywood is a village near London whose population has increased steadily since the middle of the nineteenth century. The map below shows the development of the village.

Write a report for a university lecturer describing the development of the village.

Write at least 150 words.

Village of Chorleywood showing development between 1868 and 1994

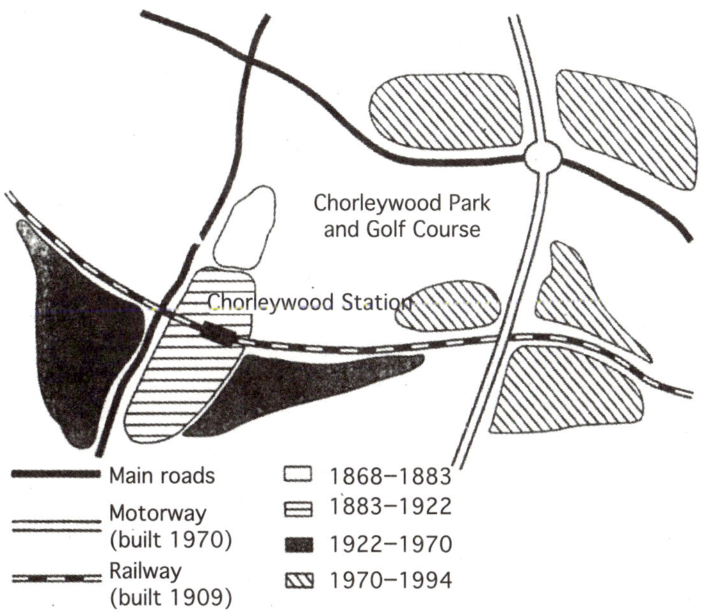

Sample Answer

This map illustrates the development of Chorleywood, a small village near London, from 1868 to 1994.

According to the map, we see that Chorleywood was only a very small area and had two crossing main roads in 1868. Not until 1883 did there emerge another habitation to the south of the original small area, which was almost twice bigger than the former one. In 1909, a railway, parallel with the eastbound main road, came into being. It went through the new habitation and formed an intersection with another main road as well. From 1922 to 1970, along the southern part of the newly-built railway, two large areas took shape. 1970 saw another great change in Chorleywood. A southbound motorway was built to link the railway and the eastbound main road. Since then, another five living areas were founded, scattering along the motorway.

Thanks to the construction of the railway and the motorway, the land of Chorleywood expanded significantly.

第五章　信函类写作

一、概述

（一）字数和时间要求

雅思写作考试普通类的第一篇是要求写一封信，字数在 150 词以上，建议用时 20 分钟。

（二）写作格式

与议论文相同，书信的段落格式有两种：缩进式和齐头式。但与议论文不同的是，写信还要有称呼和落款。称呼和落款有如下三种形式。

1．不知道收信人的姓名，甚至不知道性别，可以这样写：

Dear Sir/Madam,

…

Yours sincerely,

Fan Yang

2．知道收信人的姓名，但并不熟悉此人，可以这样写：

Dear Mr. Wang,

…

Yours sincerely,

Fan Yang

3．收信人是你的朋友或亲戚等比较熟悉的人，可以这样写：

Dear Michael,

…

Yours sincerely,

Fan

另外要注意，称呼都不向右缩进，都是齐头的。如果中间段落采用缩进式，落款应写在右下角，如果采用齐头式，则落款也应是齐头的。

下面给出书信正确格式和错误格式的范例，Sample 1 和 Sample 2 为正确格式，Sample 3 为错误格式。

Sample 1

Dear Sir/Madam,

I am writing to seek accommodation in the Snowy Mountains for a group of students from Perth.

We expect to be in the Snowy Mountains between June 1st and June 12th. There are fourteen people in our group, five men and seven women, and a married couple. The five men will accept dormitory accommodation, and the women are happy to share rooms, but the married couple would like a double room. We hope to keep our expenses as low as possible.

Please tell me about recreational services in the area. The group will bring their own boots for bushwalking, but we are hoping to hire equipment for other sports, like skiing. Some in our group will want to hire geological picks and other equipment, if possible. We also need to know about access to caves and other interesting geological features in the area.

I am looking forward to receiving information about the Student Hostel Services and other facilities.

Yours sincerely,
Fan Yang

Sample 2

Dear Sir/Madam,

I am writing to seek accommodation in the Snowy Mountains for a group of students from Perth.

We expect to be in the Snowy Mountains between June 1st and June 12th. There are fourteen people in our group, five men and seven women, and a married couple. The five men will accept dormitory accommodation, and the women are happy to share rooms, but the married couple would like a double room. We hope to keep our expenses as low as possible.

Please tell me about recreational services in the area. The group will bring their own boots for bushwalking, but we are hoping to hire equipment for other sports, like skiing. Some in our group will want to hire geological picks and other equipment, if possible. We also need to know about access to caves and other interesting geological features in the area.

I am looking forward to receiving information about the Student Hostel Services and other facilities.

Yours sincerely,
Fan Yang

Sample 3

Dear Sir/Madam,

I am writing to seek accommodation in the Snowy Mountains for a group of students from Perth.

We expect to be in the Snowy Mountains between June 1st and June 12th. There are fourteen people in our group, five men and seven women, and a married couple. The five men will accept dormitory accommodation, and the women are happy to share rooms, but the married couple would like a double room. We hope to keep our expenses as low as possible.

Please tell me about recreational services in the area. The group will bring their own boots for bushwalking, but we are hoping to hire equipment for other sports, like skiing. Some in our group will want to hire geological picks and other equipment, if possible. We also need in know about access to caves and other interesting geological features in the area.

I am looking forward to receiving information about the Student Hostel Services and other facilities.

Yours sincerely,
Fan Yang

说明：

由于采用缩进式，落款应在信的右下角。所以，Sample 3 的格式是错误的。

二、各种信函的结构

信函的正文部分一般分为三至四段：开头段和结尾段各一段，主体段落可分为一至两段。各种信函的开头段写法差不多，一般有如下三种写法：

1. 先介绍背景，然后说明写信的目的；

2. 先说明写信的目的，然后介绍背景；
3. 只说明写信的目的，把背景放在主体段落去说。

下面分别介绍各种信函的写法，每种信函的开头段的写法就不作介绍了，只介绍主体段落和结尾段的写法。每种类型的信函给出了几篇范文以供大家参考学习。

（一）抱怨信

抱怨信是考得最多的一类信函，大概占 30% 左右的比例。

主体段落一般包括：
1. 介绍背景；
2. 出现的问题、抱怨的原因；
3. 给自己带来的不便和麻烦。

结尾段一般包括：
1. 提出公平的解决方案；
2. 表示感谢；
3. 提出建议。

请看下面的范文。

Topic 1　抱怨产品质量

You should spend about 20 minutes on this task.

You have bought an MP3 at a shop. On reaching home, you discover a fault with it.

Write a letter to the shop authority explaining the situation, and ask that the problem be put right.

Write at least 150 words.

You do **NOT** need to write any address.
Begin your letter as follows:

Dear ________,

Sample Answer

Dear Sir/Madam,

I wish to make a complaint about an MP3 which I bought three days ago in your shop.

As is my habit, I made a point of trying it out on the spot. It worked well, and so I went ahead and purchased it. However, when I got home and tried it again, it seemed that the volume knob had ceased to work. Removing the back of the case, I found that the internal components of the MP3 had all rusted. Not only that but some of the wires were broken.

I am sure that you will agree that this is a most unsatisfactory situation. Therefore, I request you to arrange to replace this MP3 with another one, which must be in perfect working order. Failing that, I will have to visit for a full refund.

Yours sincerely,

Fan Yang

Topic 2 抱怨服务质量

You should spend about 20 minutes on this task.

You booked a two-week holiday to Sydney with Holiday Travel. You are not happy with the holiday—no one met you at the airport, the hotel was unsatisfactory, and so on.

Write to Holiday Travel to complain about the holiday giving details about the problems. Request some compensation or refund.

Write at least 150 words.

You do **NOT** need to write your own address.
Begin your letter as follows:

Dear ________,

Sample Answer

Dear Mr. Smith,

I am writing to complain about my recent holiday in Sydney which was organised by your company.

My wife and I selected the two-week tour starting on 29th December. On arrival at the airport, there was no one to meet us. We waited for half an hour and then had no choice but to take a taxi. This cost $30. The receipt is enclosed.

The hotel was not what I would consider three-star. The room was dirty; the beds were small and uncomfortable, and the hotel refused to provide us with dinner. We had to spend a further $500 on extra meals. Again, I enclose our restaurant receipts.

I find it dishonest and unacceptable that your company sold us a tour which in no way resembled the description, and my wife and I expect to be compensated for all our extra expenses. The receipts which are enclosed total $530. We expect to receive your cheque very soon.

Yours sincerely,
Fan Yang

Topic 3 抱怨房屋问题

You should spend about 20 minutes on this task.

You rent a house through an agency. The heating system has stopped working. You phoned the agency a week ago but it has not been mended yet.

Write a letter to the agency. Explain the situation and tell them what you want them to do about it.

Write at least 150 words.

You do **NOT** need to write your own address.
Begin your letter as follows:

Dear ________,

Sample Answer

Dear Sir/Madam,

I am, at present, living in a house which I rented through your agency. I am sorry to inform you that the heating system in the house stopped working some time ago.

I phoned your agency and explained the problem one week ago, but you have not sent anybody to fix the heating system yet. This is very inconvenient—not to mention the dangerous to health—as the weather is starting to get colder. I am puzzled as to why you have not paid attention to this urgent matter.

I must remind you that a fully operative heating system is one of the terms of the lease of the house.

Therefore, I would very much appreciate it if you would send a technician to repair the system as soon as possible. He may call at any time during the day, as either I or my wife will be at home all this week.

Yours sincerely,

Fan Yang

（二）说明信

主体段落一般包括：

1. 介绍背景；
2. 说明情况。

结尾段根据不同的题目，可以表达抱怨、感谢、表扬、道歉等语气，但不要过分渲染。

请看下面的范文。

Topic 4 说明请假原因

You should spend about 20 minutes on this task.

You have had an accident and are in hospital.

Write a letter to your college administration explaining why you will be absent from class for the next month. Ask for advice about how to continue your studies during this period.

Write at least 150 words.

You do **NOT** need to write your own address.
Begin your letter as follows:

Dear ________,

Sample Answer

Dear Prof. Smith,

I am writing to explain my absence from classes since April 21st, 1999.

On April 20th, 1999, I was involved in a serious motor vehicle accident. I was transported to the hospital in an ambulance, where I was treated for a broken ankle, fractured collarbone, and three bruised ribs. My doctor advised complete bed rest for six weeks, and as a result, I have been unable to attend classes since April 21st, 1999.

I am concerned about keeping up with my studies, and have been doing the required readings, as assigned by my professors. My biggest concern is whether I will be eligible to take the final exams in June. Would you please give me some advice regarding my courses and exams, specifically any special consideration given to me in light of my current situation?

Thank you for your kind assistance. I look forward to hearing from you soon.

Sincerely,

Fan Yang

Topic 5 说明物品丢失

You should spend about 20 minutes on this task.

You have lost your credit card.

Write to the manager of your bank. Explain where and how you lost the card and any other relevant details. Ask the manager to cancel the old card and to send you a replacement.

Write at least 150 words.

You do **NOT** need to write your own address.
Begin your letter as follows:

Dear ________,

Sample Answer

Dear Sir/Madam,

I am writing to confirm the loss of my credit card.

The details of my card are as follows. It is a Visa card in the name of Fan Yang. The credit card number is 4531 7602 2597 ××××. I have had the card since 1994. This card is valid from August 2005 to August 2006.

I lost the card at about 10:30 in the evening yesterday. The only time I used the card yesterday was to buy three dictionaries at the Haidian Bookstore. By accident, I left the card at the shop. When I realised what I had done, I telephoned the shop, but the shop assistants there could not find the card.

Could you please cancel my card immediately and make the necessary arrangements to issue me with a replacement card?

Thank you for your assistance.

Yours faithfully,

Fan Yang

（三）咨询信

咨询信是考得比较多的另一种类型的信函。

主体段落一般包括：

1. 介绍背景；
2. 自我介绍；
3. 询问详情。

结尾段一般包括：

1. 表示感谢；
2. 期待回信；
3. 询问进一步的信息。

请看下面的范文。

Topic 6 咨询出国留学的信息

You should spend about 20 minutes on this task.

Assume that you wish to study in England.

Write a letter of inquiry based on your interests. Ask what kind of clubs there are at the university, and what is the procedure for joining them.

Write at least 150 words.

You do **NOT** need to write your own address.
Begin your letter as follows:

Dear ________,

Sample Answer

Dear Sir/Madam,

I have applied to enter your esteemed university to follow a course of study. However, although I find the academic curriculum suitable, I feel that the opportunities for leisure activities are also an important part of student life. Therefore, I would be grateful if you could give me some information about this aspect of the campus.

In my spare time, I indulge myself in a wide range of sports; I am also interested in music, especially playing the guitar. Specifically, I wish to know if there are any sports clubs, including soccer and tennis teams run by students. Furthermore, I would be keen to join a student band or orchestra, if there is one.

Please write and let me know what university clubs I am eligible to join. By the way, what is the procedure for joining campus clubs, what qualifications do I need, and what are the fees for taking part in their activities?

I look forward to your reply.

Yours sincerely,
Fan Yang

Topic 7 咨询展览会的信息

You should spend about 20 minutes on this task.

As part of a student social survey project, you are organising a group to visit a historical exhibition in a small town.

Write a letter to the exhibition organiser asking for information regarding such things as the contents of the exhibition, and the dates of its opening and closing, and if there are any discounts available.

Write at least 150 words.

You do **NOT** need to write your own address.
Begin your letter as follows:

Dear ________,

Sample Answer

Dear Sir/Madam,

I am organising a group of students to pay a visit to the historical exhibition in your town. This visit will be part of our school's activities to encourage our students to take part in social surveys. Therefore, I would be grateful if you would supply me with the following information.

First of all, what are the opening and closing dates between which the exhibition will be held, and what are the daily opening hours? Secondly, what is the size of the exhibition, what is its theme and what objects are on display? Thirdly, are there any other activities being held in connection with the exhibition?

I should let you know that I hope to bring over 100 students to the exhibition. So I would like to inquire if there is any discount available on entrance tickets for students. If so, how much is the discount and what is the minimum number of students necessary to qualify for it?

I look forward to your reply.

Yours sincerely,

Fan Yang

（四）道歉信

主体段落一般包括：

1. 介绍背景；
2. 说明原因；
3. 提出弥补措施。

结尾段一般是再次道歉。

请看下面的范文。

Topic 8 道歉信

You should spend about 20 minutes on this task.

One of your pen pals will shortly be visiting your city. For some reasons, you cannot manage to meet him at the airport on time.

Write a letter asking him to wait for you at the airport and tell him how to identify you.

Write at least 150 words.

You do **NOT** need to write your own address.
Begin your letter as follows:

Dear ________,

Sample Answer

Dear David,

I am very much looking forward to your visit to my city. After all these years of writing to each other, we will finally have the chance to meet! However, I regret to inform you that I will not be able to meet you at the airport when you arrive.

I was glad to hear that you would come to see me and I thought I must go to the airport to meet you. But yesterday I was informed that I must attend an important business meeting on the day when you arrive. The meeting is supposed to be over at 11:00 a.m., which will be an hour later than your arrival time.

Please wait for me in the arrival lounge. I'll go there as quickly as possible after the meeting. As we have never met I must tell you how to recognise me: I am of medium height and have a small mustache. In addition, I will be carrying a copy of the morning newspaper tucked under my left arm.

Looking forward to our first meeting.

Yours sincerely,

Fan

（五）感谢信

主体段落一般包括：

1. 介绍背景；
2. 得到帮助前的困境；
3. 得到的帮助；
4. 带来的好处。

结尾段一般是再次表示感谢。

请看下面的范文。

Topic 9 感谢信

You should spend about 20 minutes on this task.

You have just arrived in the city where you are going to spend two years for your master's degree. You have a lot of preparation to do before the new term starts, but you do not know how to go around the city. A friend you have newly acquainted offers you guidance and helps you through difficulties.

Write a letter to express your thanks.

Write at least 150 words.

You do **NOT** need to write your own address.
Begin your letter as follows:

Dear ________,

Sample Answer

Dear David,

I am writing this letter to thank you for the guidance you gave me.

I was a perfect stranger when arriving at this city. Once I lost myself for not knowing the way in a downtown street, although I stopped to ask some people for direction. The streets and shops puzzled me so much that I would rather stay indoors. At that time, you came to see me and brought me a map of the city. You also spent a lot of your valuable time showing me around the city. Now I begin to know how to take the proper buses. Yesterday I went downtown with some of my schoolmates to buy some stationery.

Although nowadays many people talk about the need to be warmhearted and to help others, we see very few people practising what they preach. But you showed by your unselfish action that you are an exception. If there were more people like you, this world would be a much nicer place.

Best wishes and thanks again!

Yours sincerely,

Fan

三、各种信函的常用句式

（一）抱怨信

1. I am afraid that I have a complaint to make.
2. I am, at present, living in a house which I rented through your agency.
3. I am not at all satisfied with...
4. I am not satisfied with...
5. I am puzzled as to why you have not paid attention to this urgent matter.
6. I am really annoyed about it.
7. I am regretted to say that something was wrong.
8. I am sorry to inform you that...
9. I am sure that you will agree that this is a most unsatisfactory situation. Therefore, I request you to arrange to replace... Failing that, I will have to insist on a full refund.
10. I am writing to complain about...
11. I am writing to inform you that I wish to move into a new room next term.

12. I am writing to you because I am unable to pay next month's rent which is due on Saturday.
13. I am writing to you to complain about the food and the service.
14. I do wish you could.
15. I expect to hear from you very soon.
16. I feel something should be done about...
17. I find it dishonest and unacceptable that...
18. I hate to bring this up, but...
19. I have had enough of that.
20. I must complain about...
21. I must explain that the reason for my dissatisfaction is that...
22. I must remind you that...
23. I phoned your agency and explained the problem one week ago, but you have not sent anybody to...
24. I want to complain in the strongest term about...
25. I wish you would look into the matter for me and talk to the person responsible for this mistake.
26. I would be most grateful if you would...
27. I would like to point out that...
28. I'm sorry to trouble you but I'm afraid I have to make a serious complaint against one of your assistants about his bad service.
29. I'm writing to complain about...
30. I'm writing to complain that...
31. I'm writing to place a complaint against...
32. In these circumstances, I find it difficult to...
33. It didn't work properly but I couldn't find the problem.
34. It is hard for me to understand...
35. On arrival at the airport, there was no one to meet us.
36. Please change a new one for me. Otherwise, I would ask you to give my money back, or I would complain to the Consumers' Association.
37. Please give this matter your immediate attention.
38. Since we feel we should be compensated somehow, we ask you to refund the cost of...
39. Something must be done about it.
40. That is no excuse.
41. There is something you could help me with.

42. Therefore, I would be grateful if you could...
43. Therefore, I would very much appreciate it if you would...as soon as possible.

（二）咨询信

1. Could you please...?
2. Could you possibly...?
3. Could you tell me what I have to do to...?
4. First of all, what are the opening and closing dates...?
5. First of all, what facilities are available for...?
6. First, what qualifications do I need to follow for...?
7. I am anxious to obtain information about...
8. I am writing to ask for your assistance.
9. I am writing to ask if you could do/grant me a favour.
10. I am writing to express my interest in...
11. I am writing to you with a desire to...
12. I'm writing to ask you for some information as I'm planning to...
13. I look forward to your prompt response.
14. I need to have more information about...
15. I should be most obliged to you if you could...
16. I will be very much grateful if you could...
17. I wish to know if there are any...
18. I wonder if you could do...for me.
19. I would appreciate it if you would send me an application form for...
20. I would appreciate it very much if you could consider my suggestions.
21. I would be grateful if you could give me some information about...
22. I would be grateful if you would...
23. I would be grateful if you would be kind enough to...
24. I would be most grateful to you if...
25. I would like to inquire if there is...
26. I would like to meet with you at your earliest convenience, to discuss the possibility of...
27. I'm looking forward to hearing from you.
28. I'm writing because I wish to...

29. I'm writing to ask if...
30. I'm writing to explore the possibility of obtaining the position in your firm.
31. I'm writing to seek accommodation in your hotel.
32. It will be highly appreciated that/if...
33. It will be very nice of you if you could...
34. Kindly favour me with a reply at your earliest convenience.
35. Many thanks for the trouble you have taken.
36. May I...?
37. Please let me have your answer within/before (a date) as to your decision on this matter.
38. Please let me know if it is possible to...
39. Please send me all the relevant information concerning...
40. Thank you for your attention to these requests. If you have any questions, please feel free to contact me at 277-××××. I look forward to hearing from you soon.
41. Thank you for your attention to this matter.
42. Thank you for your consideration of my application. I look forward to meeting you in the near future.
43. Thank you for your consideration.
44. Thank you for your time and attention.
45. Thank you so much for your help in this matter.
46. Would it be possible to...?
47. Would you be kind enough to...?
48. Would you mind doing...?
49. Would/Could you please give/offer/send me some information about.../some materials on...?
50. Your prompt attention to this matter would be highly appreciated.
51. Your prompt response would be appreciated.

（三）感谢信

1. I am most grateful for...
2. I am very much indebted to you.
3. I am very much obliged to you.
4. I am writing to express my heartfelt gratitude.
5. I can never thank you enough./I really cannot thank you enough./I really do not know how I

can thank you enough.
6. I do appreciate your timely help.
7. I must thank you for...
8. I should like to express my appreciation.
9. I should like to express my gratitude for your kindness.
10. I should like to say how grateful I am./I am extremely grateful to you.
11. It is most thoughtful of you that.../You are very thoughtful/considerate to...
12. It is/was very good/kind of you to...
13. Many thanks for...
14. Thank you for...

（四）道歉信

1. I am afraid I have brought you too much trouble.
2. I am sorry for any inconveniences I have caused by...
3. I am writing to apologise for the abrupt way that I...
4. I cannot tell you how sorry I am.
5. I did not mean to hurt your feelings.
6. I do apologise for what I have done.
7. I do beg your pardon for the mess I have made.
8. I just do not know what to say.
9. I must apologise about (not) doing…
10. I must make an apology for losing my temper.
11. I really feel bad about that.
12. I regret to inform you that I will not be able to...
13. I was informed that the regular orientation session for new students will be held on February 25th. However, I regret to inform you that I will be unable to attend the session.
14. I'm sorry that I cannot...
15. I'm terribly sorry, but…
16. I'm writing to say sorry for...
17. It was careless of me.
18. It was really quite unintentional.
19. Once again, I am sorry for any inconvenience caused.

20. Please accept my apologies once more.
21. Please accept my sincere apologies for…
22. Please forgive my forgetfulness/negligence.

（五）说明信

1. Could you please cancel my...and make the necessary arrangements to...
2. I am writing to confirm the loss of...
3. I am writing to explain...
4. I hope this information will help you.
5. I'm writing to inform you of...
6. I'm writing to report...
7. Please feel free to contact me for more information.
8. When I arrived home I discovered that I had left one of...

（六）邀请信

1. Can you come over and join us?
2. Could we have the honour of your presence at the meeting?
3. Do you fancy coming along?
4. How about coming to...
5. I think it would be a good idea if...
6. I wonder if you could come.
7. I would very much like you to come to (our party).
8. I'd like to ask you to come.
9. I'd really like you to...
10. If you could manage, we would like you to attend...
11. Is there any chance of your coming?
12. May we have the pleasure of your company at dinner?
13. Perhaps you would care to come to a party on Saturday.
14. We should be delighted/so pleased if you could...
15. Why don't you come (on a holiday with us)?
16. Why don't you come to...

17. Would you do me the pleasure/honour of attending (our wedding ceremony)?
18. Would you honour us with a visit?
19. You must join us (for lunch).

（七）安排

1. Are you doing anything special tonight?/Do you have any plans for tonight?
2. Could you make it Friday?/Could you manage Friday?/Do you think that you could arrange for that Friday?/May I expect you to be there Friday?
3. Do you happen to be free this afternoon?
4. I wonder whether it would be convenient to meet you tomorrow afternoon.
5. I wonder whether you could arrange with me about the meeting today.
6. I wonder whether you could spare me some time this afternoon.
7. I would like (to have) an appointment for tomorrow afternoon.
8. I would like to drop by today to talk over the contract.
9. I would like to fix an appointment with you.
10. I'm planning...
11. I'm thinking of...
12. I've arranged to...
13. May I make an appointment with you?
14. Will it be convenient if I call on you at seven?
15. Will you be occupied/free/busy this afternoon?

（八）建议

1. Could you please...
2. I am of the opinion that...is qualified to do/for...
3. I consider...a very dedicated professional. He would be highly eligible to fill the position.
4. I feel very safe in recommending...to you.
5. I have found...to be a hard-working person, who has made some outstanding achievements/success/accomplishments/fulfillment.
6. I hope these suggestions will be helpful. But if I can help in any other way, please let me know.
7. I know...to have been a promising (student/employee) of intelligence and ability.

8. I strongly recommend...
9. I take pleasure in recommending to you...
10. I trust these suggestions have been useful.
11. I was very pleased to hear...and hope the following information will help you to...
12. I'd like to suggest that...
13. It will be greatly appreciated if you will give...a chance to...
14. May I suggest that...
15. Not only I myself but also my colleagues shall deem it a great favour if you will give... assistance guidance.
16. Perhaps we could...
17. Please let me know if I can help any further.